MEMORY LANE

# Guildford
# & District

*MEMORY LANE*

# Guildford & District

by David Rose

The Breedon Books
Publishing Company
Derby

First published in Great Britain by

The Breedon Books Publishing Company Limited

Breedon House, Unit 3, Parker Centre, Derby DE21 4SZ.

2000

ISBN 1 85983 194 X

Printed and bound by Butler & Tanner Ltd., Selwood Printing Works, Caxton Road, Frome, Somerset.

Colour separations and jacket printing by GreenShires Group Ltd, Leicester.

# Contents

With love to
Bryony Fleur.

# Introduction

The power of nostalgia and local history cannot be understated; whether it is simply a sentimental journey into one's past or a serious study of how our forebears lived.

In this new millennium it seems that more and more of us enjoy a glimpse of days gone by and the history on our doorstep. Fortunately, for Guildfordians, there is a wealth of information waiting to be discovered.

When Graham Collyer and I wrote *Images of Guildford* we suggested that the pictures included in that book were just the 'tip of an iceberg' of others hidden away in the collections of individuals and organisations. This has indeed proved to be true. Over the last two years I have added considerably to my own collection of picture postcard views of Guildford and the surrounding district. I have met or corresponded with many people who have, in greater or lesser amounts, collections of hitherto rarely seen photographs of the town spanning the last 140 years. I would like to take this opportunity to thank these people who have allowed me to reproduce their pictures and those who have supplied information for this book.

The cover picture, plus others of the town centre in the 1960s through to the 1970s, including the fire at the Royal Grammar School, were taken by John Sutton. Peter Bullen, who once owned Past Delights, an antiques and collectables shop in Chapel Street, provided some rare Edwardian picture postcard views, as did postcard collector and dealer Graham Richardson. Matthew Alexander and Eric Hunter of Guildford Museum helped with some of the Victorian views, while Norman Hamshere allowed me the pick of his many railway and bus photographs.

The collection of picture postcards owned by Joanne Harle and her father, Ivor Merritt, afforded some excellent material including the fabulous picture of the Friary Brewery which forms the front endpaper.

Stan Newman has been collecting information on old Guildford for many years and since the 1970s has been photographing buildings shortly before their demolition. A number of his pictures are featured including some of Guildford's 'lost pubs'.

Others who have loaned pictures and helped with information include:

The *Surrey Advertiser*, Surrey History Centre, Margaret Blythman, Margaret Brady, John Butcher, Syd Mosdell, Tom Wilkie, Ann Tizard, Albert Carter, Peter Trevaskis, John and Brenda Wakefield, Pearl Edwards, Helen Russell, Ann Pennifold, Colin Fletcher, Evelyn Comley, Doris Butler, Craig Phillips and Mary Griffiths of the Guildford Division of St John Ambulance, Jo Dwyer, Doreen Collins, Rosemary Povey, Mary Elton, Mr P. J. Fisher, Freda Morgan, Dinah Webb, Ted Mills, Jack Kinghorn, Peter Quittenton, John Black, Mick Fisher, Neil Charman, May Gould, Bernard Parke, Clive Wicks, Neil Davis, Barrie Nurse, John Corpes, Barry Talman, George Gaff, Marion May, Richard Jackson, John Yorke, Richard Ford, Mrs Searle and Phyllis Eamer. My apologies go to anyone not named whose pictures have been used and who it has not been possible to contact.

I would like to thank my parents who have lived in Guildford all their lives and have answered many of my question about 'the old days'. Thanks also go to my contemporary historians and those before me whose published works have been vital to my knowledge of Guildford. I would like to thank in particular, Mark Sturley. His book, *The Breweries and Public Houses of Guildford*, is, without doubt, my favourite book.

The first five chapters of *Memory Lane Guildford and District* deal largely with the town itself and follow one another in chronological order. Where possible the pictures in each chapter follow in date order, although occasionally pictures have been grouped to their geographical location.

Although no one will have memories of the mid-Victorian era, recollections of Guildford in those days will have been passed down through successive generations and on this period much has been written. It is therefore important to include here pictures from the 19th century and the early days of photography.

Strictly speaking, the Edwardian period ended when George V succeeded Edward VII in 1910. However, it is often acknowledged that the era continued until the end of World War One, after which life in Britain changed considerably. For this book, the Edwardian chapter follows that doctrine. The golden age in the chapter's title refers to what is recognised as the heyday of the picture postcard.

Many memories should come flooding back in the next three chapters – the 1920s-40s, the 1950s-60s, and the 1970s-80s. They show many of the changes that have taken place in and around the town that most readers will themselves remember.

Buildings in the High Street have been renumbered on more than one occasion. Street numbers referred to in the captions are those of the date of the photograph.

It was a difficult task choosing the places which make up, for this book anyway, the district of Guildford. Parishes, wards and villages have merged and changed over the years (Stoughton and Stoke in particular). One person's idea of a boundary line will almost certainly differ from the next person. Also there is, inevitably, the occasional cross over with streets and buildings and so on, seen in the earlier chapters. However, I have tried to feature places that are in close proximity of the town and with close links to it. The choice was also determined to some extent by the availability of photographs and information at the time.

I very much hope you enjoy this journey down memory lane.

David Rose
**Summer 2000**

Front endpaper: A panoramic view of Friary, Holroyd & Healy's Brewery Ltd seen here from the roof of the Quadrant buildings in Bridge Street. Note the ornate street lighting and the advertising hoardings. Today the site is occupied by the Friary shopping centre.

Back endpaper: A post-Second World War view of the High Street from the tower of St Nicolas Church.

Photograph of author (jacket flap) Ashley Prytherch.

# A Victorian Town by the River Wey

A group of people have appeared while the Victorian photographer sets up his equipment. Someone moved while the photograph was being taken and appears blurred on the resultant image. Castle Arch, facing on to Quarry Street, dates from the 13th century and is made of a very hard form of chalk known as clunch.

The façade of the Angel Hotel looks much the same today as it did about 130 years ago. The posting house and the livery stable signs hark back to an era before the railways when horse-drawn coaches passed through the town. In 1839, for example, the Independent coach stopped at the Angel every Tuesday, Thursday and Saturday en route to London from Chichester. The Red Rover called at the Crown Hotel, while the Hero stopped at the White Lion Hotel on its way to Brighton.

A rather peaceful view of the High Street in about 1865. This was certainly not the case 10 years earlier when the annual Bonfire Night riots by the Guildford Guys were in full swing. As darkness fell each November 5, a huge bonfire was lit outside Holy Trinity Church. Fireworks were let off and the mob would rampage through the town attacking passers by and damaging property. Despite numerous efforts by the civic dignitaries, police, militia and the army, it was not until 1864 that the rioting finally ceased.

For many years Guildford was served by two police forces – the Surrey Constabulary and the Borough Police Force. Here are members of the former outside their headquarters in Woodbridge Road in about 1867. The man in the centre wearing the 'pillbox hat' is Roger Parke who by that time was an inspector. The man in the bowler hat was the force's detective.

Charles Mandeville, who had been one of Guildford's watchmen, became a constable when the Borough Police Force was formed in 1836. Police historian Richard Ford says that there was once a distinction between 'night constables' and 'day policemen'. Mandeville, who wore the number 1 on his collar, was a 'night constable' on account of his former nocturnal experiences.

The ill-fated St Nicolas Church that only lasted from 1837 to 1874. Designed by Robert Ebbels, it was of poor quality and the roof leaked. In 1871 the Rev Dr John Monsell became rector and set about replacing it. The present church was consecrated in April 1876.

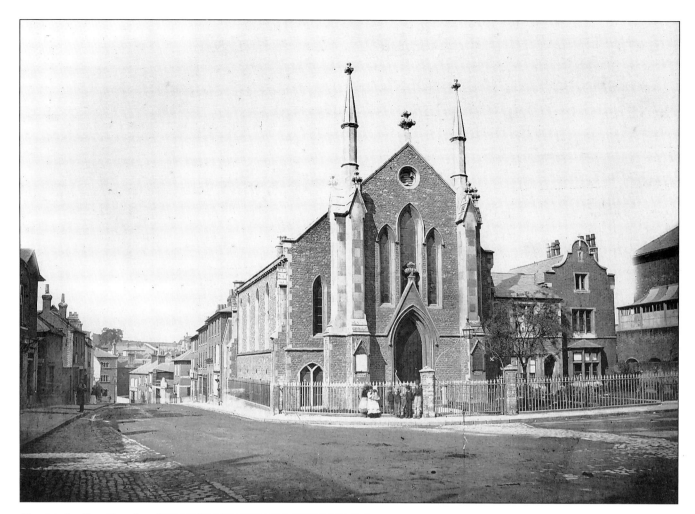

The Methodist Church in North Street in the 1860s. It was built in 1844 only to be demolished in 1892 when a larger church was constructed on the site at the corner of Woodbridge Road.

A farmer rides his horse down the High Street and sheep pens cover the roadway on market day. It was held here until 1865 when it transferred to North Street.

Farmers in North Street opposite the Surrey Arms public house. The sheep in their pens are a reminder of the 13th-century local woollen industry which made Guildford a wealthy town. Cloth was dyed with woad to produce a colour known as Guildford blue. It was then laid out to dry on racks or frames which have given their name to Racks Close.

Look carefully and you should be able to work out where this 1860s view is. It is in fact Woodbridge Road and some of the buildings still survive near what is now the Forger and Firkin public house, which was built as the Drummond Arms in 1852.

There is a house in Stoke Road that looks very similar to the one pictured here in about the 1860s. The men appear to be wearing their finest top hats and tails and the women's dresses look to be of a similar quality.

Travellers in and out of Guildford on the Portsmouth Road once had to pass through the toll-gate that stood near Guildown. The road was 'turnpiked' in 1749 and this photo shows it in its last years before it was removed in 1870, by which time the railways had won the day in the battle for both passenger and goods trade.

The railway came to Guildford in the form of a branch line from Woking laid by the London & South Western Railway Company. The station opened on May 5, 1845, and was a terminus for four years until the line was extended to Godalming. Havant and a connection to Portsmouth was not reached until 1859. Here we see the station in the late 1860s, by which time trains of the South Eastern Railway were servicing the station on the Reading to Redhill route. For a while it was called Guildford Junction.

Guildford expanded thanks to the direct influence of the railways. On October 2, 1865, the London, Brighton & South Coast Railway arrived with its branch line from Horsham. Although the original photograph is not dated, it is likely that this scene was the opening day of the service to Horsham. On the left are the Guildford Rifle Volunteers wearing their grey uniforms.

The original station buildings had roofs spanning the railway lines. With not a train in sight, the station staff appear to have little to do. The station was re-built in the 1880s and again in the 1980s.

In the 1850s, with trouble brewing in Europe, Britain revived its militia. Barracks were built in Friary Street for the volunteers who formed the 2nd Surrey Militia. The entrance was through a low arch. Above it was a tablet with the motto 'Salvam Domine Fac Victoriam' – O Lord save Victoria. The militia became part of the Queen's Royal West Surrey Regiment in 1876. The depot was eventually used for housing and businesses.

Workers at Filmer & Mason's Iron Foundry at Millmead in the 1860s. It made castings for agricultural implements as well as domestic items. However, cheaper mass-produced goods from the industrial north saw to the decline of the Guildford foundry. The last furnace was put out in about 1941, at which time it was under the ownership of Dickenson & Burne.

A view of St Mary's Church from Millmead in about 1870. To the right is the iron foundry. The agricultural vehicles are probably waiting to be repaired.

The photographer has climbed to the top of St Catherine's to take this picture looking across Guildown to Booker's Tower on the horizon. This is one of several in this chapter taken by J. Chaplin whose studio was at 2 Lea Pale Road, Guildford.

The foot of St Catherine's hill and the ferry crossing. These four photographs date from about 1865 and are quite remarkable when it is realised what went into taking them. Not only did Chaplin have to cart his bulky camera up the hill, but his processing equipment too.

Views from St Catherine's hill with the River Wey meandering through Shalford Meadows. Once Chaplin's photo shoot was over the glass plates were carefully taken back to his studio where his brother printed the photographs on to stiff cardboard.

A bend in the river that affords as charming a view today as it did here in about 1870, although much has changed. We see the form

olly Farmer public house and boathouse while the hill beyond and sides of the chalk quarry are devoid of trees.

This is Tumbling Bay at Millmead, and like many of Chaplin's photographs was printed in sepia on to small cards measuring 4in x 2.5in (102mm x 63mm). Known as cartes-de-visites, they were the invention of Andre Disderi, a French photographer and author, who patented this quick and cheap process in 1854. They were designed to be given away as souvenirs. Victorians filled leather-bound photo albums with these views.

The County and Borough Halls in North Street photographed soon after they were built in 1861. They had many functions including hosting the County Assizes and Petty Sessions as well as being home to the town's post office between 1870 and 1886.

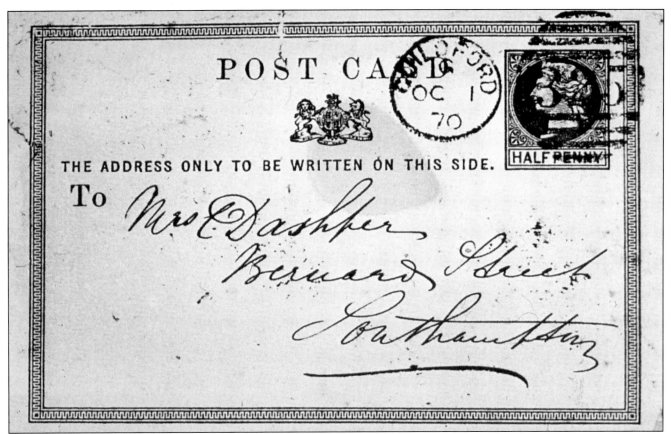

An amazing piece of postal history with a Guildford connection. The postcard as we know it was first issued in the Austro-Hungarian Empire in 1869. Exactly a year later Britain followed suit. Printed on buff coloured card with an imprinted purple half penny stamp, one side was for the address of the recipient, the other side for the message. Picture postcards were not issued until the autumn of 1894.

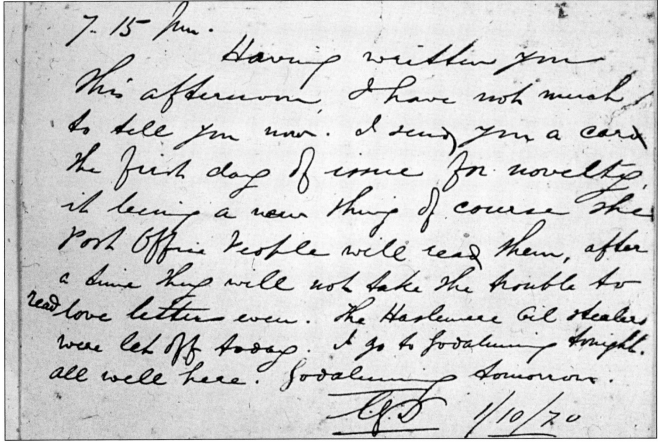

So here we have a postcard sent from Guildford to an address in Southampton on their first day of issue – October 1, 1870. The message too is remarkable, mentioning this new form of unsealed communication with the comment that 'after a time they (post office staff) will not take the trouble to read love letters even'.

The Royal Surrey County Hospital in Farnham Road opened in 1866 and none other than Florence Nightingale herself was consulted for her opinions when the wards were being designed.

The Portsmouth Road towards Artington. Here, during the middle of the 19th century, substantial homes were being built. This is how it looked in the late 1860s.

The architects' department of the Friary Brewery once occupied these buildings in Commercial Road. The view looks towards Woodbridge Road, which is on the far right.

Wellington Place in Woodbridge Road in about 1870. Vegetables are being grown in the vacant plot opposite.

Navies working on the New Line – the Guildford to Waterloo via Cobham route – at the site of London Road railway station in 1882. This area later became a goods yard. The embankment on the right remains but the goods yard itself (in the left foreground) was sold off by British Railways for housing in the late 1980s.

The date is June 9, 1896, and the view shows the final cattle market to be held in North Street before being transferred to a site at Woodbridge Road. The picture was taken from a window of the Crown public house, that stood next to the Cloth Hall.

With roads named after eminent Victorian physicians, Charlotteville was the brainchild of Thomas Sells, a Guildford doctor. He acted as the entrepreneur for this estate but it was actually designed by Henry Peak, with the first homes going up in 1862. Dr Sells named it after his wife, Charlotte. This view shows Addison Road in about 1900.

The Barley Mow public house was on the corner of Park Street and the Mount, only a stone's throw from Crooke's Brewery which supplied it. The enamel advertising sign below the centre window is for The People newspaper, boasting that it had 140 columns. Although altered, the building still stands but the pub itself closed before World War One.

A heavily-laden horse and cart is passing the Greyhound public house just over the town bridge. On the right is the Connaught Family and Commercial Hotel, which was demolished in 1942. The Greyhound is now called the George Abbot.

No way through: the February 1900 floods swept timber from Moons yard into the town bridge damaging it beyond repair. It was two years before the new bridge was opened.

# The Edwardian Golden Age

Although Edward VII became King on January 22, 1901, his coronation did not take place until August 9 the following year. In Guildford an arch was erected at Ram Corner to commemorate the event. Along with other shops, Quittenton's umbrella business hung up banners and flags.

The Great Storm of August 2, 1906, which claimed two lives and wreaked havoc across the town, has been well documented. However, this picture is quite rare. It shows the Avenue (now Woodbridge Road near its junction with Stocton Road to the right). The children appear to be gathering fire wood and workmen are repairing the tiles on one of the roofs. The fatalities at this spot were Ruth Blunden, aged 23 and Charles Voice, 14. His brother, Alfred, survived but suffered serious concussion caused by the fallen trees.

First job is to get the tree out of the bedroom! Park Cottages along Shalford Road felt the brunt of the Great Storm. Amazingly, no-one was seriously injured here.

The old smithy in the upper High Street shortly before it closed in 1906. It was run by the Lymposs family who were also dairymen. Many Guildfordians will remember having their milk delivered by Lymposs & Smee. It's hard to imagine where this ramshackle building once stood, but today the site is occupied by shops, a few doors up from McDonald's fast food restaurant.

# BATCHELOR'S

### HAIRCUTTING AND ❧
### ❧ SHAVING SALOON.

#### Guildford's Oldest Tradesman, also a Local Historian, in his 87th year.

CARRYING on his profession, as an Improver of the personal appearance of the Phizogs of His Majesty's Subjects, and who would thank many more friends to pay him a visit to let him Cut their Hair or smooth their chins, which he can do as easy and clean as he did 70 years ago; then why should not a few more friends give him a trial? either for him to Grind or Set their Razors, or to Doctor and Cure their Umbrellas from their many Ailments, of Bruised Skins, Broken Ribs and Spreaders, or new Cover them to keep off the Heavenly dew. Just to assist the old Veteran over the stile and another step or two up the Difficult Ladder of Life—the above operations are attended to daily, without the aid of Beecham's Pills, or Mother Seigel's Syrup.

P.S.—Russell's Guildford Almanack for 1845, (62 years ago) contains 557 names of its then Inhabitants. It is a Remarkable Fact that in August, 1907, BATCHELOR, ALLEN, is the Only Man Living out of the list, to tell the tale.

#### NOTE THE ADDRESS:
## 3, CHERTSEY STREET,
(Next door to H. Fentum Phillips & Co.'s Enterprising, Attractive, Brilliant, Electric Light, and Showy Golden Lion).

A 1907 advertisement for Batchelor's Haircutting and Shaving Saloon. Mr Batchelor, in his 87th year at the time claims, among many things, to be Guildford's oldest tradesman and historian.

Love may have been in the air when the the Tyrolean giantess, Miss Marie Fassnauer, 8ft 4in, arrived in Guildford on Sunday, March 24, 1907. She was appearing at the Hippodrome in London and had taken a ride in a motor-car to escape the city. The *Surrey Advertiser* reported that she was being courted by Clive Darrill, 8ft 8in, of Australia. However, although he had sworn his love for her and had bought tickets to see all her shows, she, apparently, was having none of it. Marie, 27, hardly spoke a word of English but claimed that she had no desire to marry. A large crowd witnessed the scene outside the Angel Hotel where the couple met face to face for the first time and then had lunch together. As she stepped from the car – in her size 22 boots – the onlookers gasped in amazement at her height.

As part of the Empire Day celebrations on Sunday and Monday, May 24 and 25, 1908, Holy Trinity and St Mary's Schools were presented with a Union Jack by the officers and men of HMS Vernon. It was unfurled in front of a large crowd and was given in appreciation of the care received by First Class Petty Officer Tavener at the Royal Surrey County Hospital after he had been injured in a bicycle accident at Hindhead.

North Street with firemen everywhere and neither a blaze nor a wisp of smoke. The occasion is thought to be Hospital Saturday, that took place on July 4, 1908. It was a fundraising event for charitable institutions. Guildford Fire Brigade, under the supervision of Captain T. Hooke and First Officer A. W. Hill, organised a series of competitions for their men which were watched by the public. A collection made £1 4s 5d (£1.22) which went towards a total of £183 6s 9 3/4d (£183.34) raised throughout the borough.

A crowd has gathered to witness a group of men scaling the four-storey building opposite the fire station in North Street. They appear to be trying out one of the ladders possibly belonging to the town's fire brigade.

Has the cyclist nipped in for a swift half or did he stay for the whole session? We will almost certainly never know but the Friary Brewery Tap public house, which stood on the corner of North Street and Swan Lane, had closed for good by about 1912. In recent times it was home to Bernards, who sold cooked meats and bacon.

Jackson's cycle shop in Portsmouth Road shortly after it had opened. This picture postcard was produced by the shop to advertise that it was trading in the town. Some of the Jackson family are pictured here and in the background can be glimpsed part of the Castle Brewery.

A little bit of history on one of the town's own historians. This is a postcard sent by Dr George Williamson. It has a picture of his study at his Guildford home, The Mount. Born in 1858 of a prosperous merchant family, George Williamson became an art historian specialising in miniatures. He mixed with Victorian high society but is remembered in Guildford for uncovering a wealth of local history. His books include *Guildford in the Olden Time* and *The Guild Hall of Guildford and its Treasures*. He founded the Old Guildford Society in 1896, the town's first conservation group. He was made Honourary Remembrancer, or the official chronicler of the town in 1933, and one of his first tasks was to make official investigations into the viability of Guildford achieving a city status. In latter years his methods and the accuracy of the historical facts he uncovered have come under some criticism.

The upper High Street seen here when the road was much narrower. The buildings on the left have disappeared but Somerset House on the right, still stands. It was built during the early part of the 18th century as a staging post for the Duke of Somerset for when he was travelling from his Petworth home to London.

The buildings known as Ram Corner, at the junction of the High Street and Chertsey Street, were pulled down in 1913 for a vital road widening scheme.

The Quittenton umbrella business came to Guildford from Reading in 1889. The first shop was at 34 Spittal Street (now upper High Street). In 1901 it transferred to Ram Corner moving again in 1908 to 154 High Street. The owner, Maurice Quittenton, and his son, Maurice Jnr, are pictured.

In 1913 they moved again, this time to number 105 and a half High Street pictured here. Quittenton's could re-cover, replace and repair any part of an umbrella. Walking sticks and toiletries were also stocked and a cutlery grinding service was available; any blade could be sharpened, from a cut-throat razor to a pair of garden shears. Maurice Snr handed over the business to his son in 1930 and it wasn't long before the shop was on the move again, this time to the Rodboro Buildings. See picture in the next chapter.

On a summer's day crowds have turned out to see a procession wend its way through the town. Here it passes over the bridge by London Road railway station.

Guildford High School was founded in 1888 in Haydon Place. Schools purely for girls were uncommon at that time and it was not until its second week that any pupils were actually enrolled. Its first headmistress was a Miss Agnes Morton. In 1893 the school moved to new buildings in London Road, seen here.

Pupils at Guildford High School with their teacher in the school's garden in the early 1900s. The girls came from middle-class families living in the Epsom Road/London Road area. Some fathers would have commuted to London by rail each day. The school magazine of the time said a father would be 'driven to the station in a comfortable brougham, well wrapped in a stout overcoat, with rugs around his knees, a camellia or some other hot house flower in his button hole, most probably placed there by the fair hands of his devoted slave – his wife'.

It took nearly 30 years to build the Royal Grammar School. It was completed in 1586 and its appearance has hardly changed. In 1512 a wealthy London grocer, Robert Beckingham, died leaving the means to finance a school in Guildford. For a while one was established in Castle Street. By 1547 it had run into financial difficulties and was then confiscated along with other charities by Edward VI. Four years later it was re-endowed by the King and in that same year the corporation acquired the land on which the present grammar school was built. Difficult times returned in the 18th century when it actually closed for a while. It was radically reorganised as a day school in 1889 and in the 1960s a much larger extension was built on the opposite side of the upper High Street where Allen House had stood.

A carefully posed picture postcard view of pupils at the Royal Grammar School, showing a woodwork class.

Two more postcards from the Royal Grammar School, this time showing the gymnasium and a science lesson in progress.

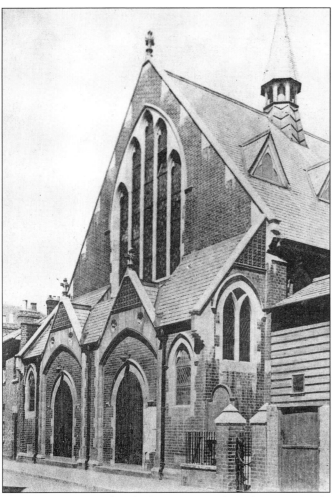

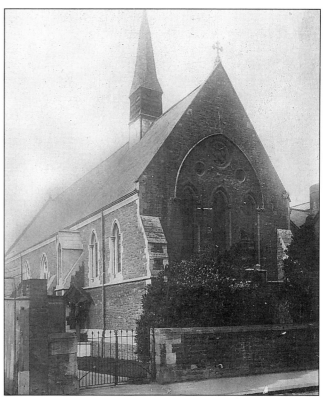

This is the Baptist Church that once stood on the eastern side of Commercial Road near its junction with North Street. The cottages to the left still stand.

St Joseph's Roman Catholic Church stood in Chertsey Street adjacent to The Bars. It was built in 1881 and pulled down in April 1982. A replacement church was built in Denmark Road and consecrated on September 8, 1984. It was hoped that the spire of the old church would be saved and used on the new building, but this was not to be. The *Surrey Times* reported in 1985 that it was to be sold to Terry Gilliam of Monty Python fame and would be placed in the garden of his Highgate mansion.

A busy market day in Woodbridge Road during the 1900s. Mind where you tread though, the road is littered with dung!

When this photograph was taken, shortly before World War One, someone by the name of J. Davies was running The Napoleon Family and Commercial Hotel, in Farnham Road. The other hotel pitching for business from travellers arriving at the station was the Railway Hotel.

Although these original steps have been replaced, a walkway linking Walnut Tree Close with Farnham Road still exists near the railway station approach.

Soldiers march from the railway station down Farnham Road. Who could fail to miss Farnham Road Ale Stores with a sign like this!

Four generations of the Crooke family brewed beer on the west bank of the River Wey by the town bridge. The brewery buildings can be seen in this view that looks upstream from Bridge Street in the 1900s. When the brewery was wound up in 1929 it had 25 licensed houses including the Castle, the Horse and Groom, the Wheatsheaf and the Greyhound in the town centre. Others were as far afield as the Three Compasses at Alfold and the Green Dragon at Liphook.

F. A. Crooke & Co. Ltd, one pint beer bottle dating from circa 1910.

The previous post office in North Street was a rather grand red-brick building. Its late-1960s replacement stands in exactly the same position.

This is how the bottom of North Street looked circa 1910. On the left is Tom Picken's Stores, near the entrance to Commercial Road. Dominating the view is the spire of the Methodist Church on the corner of Woodbridge Road.

A group of workers from the Friary Brewery in the early years of the 20th century. Note the long aprons worn by some of the women. Their work in the bottling department would have been both cold and wet.

Built on the site of a 13th century Dominican Friary, the Friary Brewery's origins go back to the Chennel family of brewers who were also millers. In the middle of the 19th century they built a flour mill on the site of the old friary. It was later acquired and converted into a brewery by the Guildford brewer Thomas Taunton who was looking to expand his business. The name Friary Brewery first appeared in the town's trade directories in 1873. In that same year Charles Hoskin Master became a partner with Taunton. Unfortunately they soon quarrelled and within a year Master had bought Taunton out. From then on the business grew. In 1889 it merged with Holroyd's Brewery of Byfleet and the following year they were joined by Healy's Brewery of Chertsey. Other local breweries were acquired, including, in 1926, Friary's main Guildford rival, Lascelles, Tickner & Co. It merged with Meux to form Friary Meux in 1956. Brewing ended in Guildford in 1969. However, the name Friary Meux has continued and can still be found on some public houses in the South of England. The picture shows three Friary stoneware jars dating from the late Victorian/early Edwardian era.

Nealds & Cooper half gallon stoneware jar circa 1900.

Wine merchants Nealds & Cooper were established in the High Street in 1775 by John Nealds, who was five times mayor. His partner, Castels Cooper, was mayor in 1843. The firm is listed in the 1892 *General Business Guide to Guildford* and this picture probably post dates that by a few years. However, the guide says:

'A large and efficient staff of hands is regularly employed, under the direction and strict personal control of Mr Mark Sheppard. Nealds & Cooper are always willing, and, indeed, anxious, to make sure that their customers get exactly what they require. In order to ensure this they engage none but first-class cellarmen and bottlers.' In 1921 the business was taken over by Henekeys.

Boots Cash Chemists in the High Street has a well stocked window. Next door, where the men are climbing a ladder, was the Jolly Butchers public house. It closed in 1929.

Boots and some local chemists sold face creams in shallow ceramic dishes with printed lids. Henry Jeffries set up in business in 1815 and Jeffries Passage is named after him.

Framing this view are two of the High Street's most impressive buildings, Holy Trinity Church and the Hospital of the Blessed Trinity (Abbot's Hospital). Note the shop front of the dairy firm Gates – later Cow & Gate– on the right and on the left, in front of the church, the hut that was a shelter for people waiting for taxis.

St Mary's Church, with its Saxon tower dating back to about 1050, is Guildford's oldest building.

We can thank the town's Victorian borough surveyor Henry Peak for designing the Castle Grounds. His plan was adopted by the corporation in 1885 and on June 28, 1888, they were formally opened. There were once greenhouses on site but today the bedding plants are raised at the borough's nurseries in Stoke Park. Nowadays, approximately 36,000 plants are used for the spring planting and a further 39,000 for the summer planting. The emphasis is on informal bedding unlike yesteryear when plants were laid out in regimental lines.

Hundreds of views of the Castle Grounds were published as picture postcards during the early years of the 20th century. This one looks towards the bowling green with the bandstand on the right. Bowls has been played here for at least 250 years. However, for a few years in the early 1900s it was stopped and the green was renamed the Mayor's Lawn. By 1907 though, the game had been re-introduced.

The first superintendent of the Castle Grounds was Charles Sanders, who took up his post when the grounds were being landscaped in 1885. He retired after 42 years service. His successor was Ted Wright who stayed in the job for over 45 years. Len Dando replaced him and was the manager of parks and open spaces until he retired in 1999.

Mystery surrounds the whereabouts of this beautiful fountain that once stood just inside the Castle Street entrance to the Castle Grounds. Made of terracotta, it was removed in about 1910 when the grounds were re-designed.

A tin church, gas lamps and trees! This is how Guildford Park Road looked about 90 years ago. The modern Guildford Park Church now occupies the site on the right, but the houses on the left look much the same.

Interior views of the old Royal Surrey County Hospital in Farnham Road are rare. However, this one shows Albert ward – presumably a men's ward – sometime between 1910-20. It was actually reproduced as a picture postcard. Not really a 'wish you were here' style of correspondence!

A panoramic view looking northwards from Racks Close. Dominating the view is St Nicolas Church and two tall chimneys. The left-hand one belonged to Lascelles Tickner & Co's Castle Brewery, at the foot of Portsmouth Road, and the other was at the Guildford Park brickworks.

Smoke rises from the chimneys of the cottages along Millmead. The building on the extreme right is the original Britannia public house. This largely wooden building was burnt to the ground in 1912, but soon re-built. It became a victim of the 1990s trend to transform traditional bars into theme pubs. The apt narrow boat-style decor for this waterside pub was replaced by a mock Irish style and it was renamed Scruffy Murphy's.

Tumbling Bay upstream from Millmead has changed very little but notice how bare Warwick's Bench looked before the developers got to work creating some of the most desirable homes in Guildford.

Paddock Gardens stood on the banks of the River Wey near Shalford Meadows and was a theatre and concert venue.

A much photographed spot on the River Wey showing Leroy's Boat House and the Jolly Farmer public house. These two views show the original pub (above) and the new one constructed in 1913. The boat house buildings were also altered during the early 1900s.

# CHARLES LEROY,

## "Jolly Farmer" Boathouse,

### Quarry Street, GUILDFORD.

FIRST-CLASS ALES, WINES, AND SPIRITS.

THIS Inn, being situate immediately on the banks of the river, possesses every facility for the equipment of

*New and Second-hand Boats and Canoes for Sale and Hire.*

## Boating Parties.

Repairs on the Shortest Notice. Oars and Sculls made to Order.
Boats Let on Hire by the Day, Month, or Year.

---

Advertisements from Guildford
Guide books of the early 1900s.

---

ESTABLISHED OVER      A CENTURY.

# FILMER & MASON,

## Furnishing Ironmongers, and

Public Buildings, Conservatories, and Baths heated on the most Approved Principles.

# MEDIÆVAL . METAL . . WORKERS,

MANUFACTURERS OF KITCHEN RANGES,

*Bellhangers, Locksmiths, and Gasfitters,*

## SANITARY ❖ ENGINEERS,

MANUFACTURERS OF WROUGHT-IRON AND STEEL

WELDED AND . .
. . . . RIVETED **BOILERS**

OF EVERY DESCRIPTION, FOR

**HOT-WATER HEATING APPARATUS,
KITCHEN RANGE BOILERS, VERTICAL STEAM BOILERS,
GAS BOILERS AND HOT-WATER VALVES.**

## WROUGHT-IRON FENCING

HURDLES AND GATES,

WIRE FENCING & TREE GUARDS, WINE BINS, TANKS, etc.

---

# SIMPSON BROS.

### (LATE JOHN SIMPSON),

## Drapers and Silk Mercers,

### FAMILY LINEN WAREHOUSE,

27 & 28, HIGH STREET,
AND 76 North Street
GUILDFORD.

AGENT FOR LIBERTY'S ART FABRICS.

## Family Mourning.

MILLINERY, MANTLES, and COSTUMES,
DRESSMAKING, LADIES' OUTFITTING, BABY LINEN, and
GENTLEMEN'S OUTFITTER.

### EVENING AND DINNER DRESSES MADE TO ORDER.

*CARPETS, LINOLEUMS,
FLOORCLOTHS, JAPANESE AND INDIAN RUGS.*

---

# F. OSTLER,

## The County Cycle & Motor Depot,

### Bridge Street, GUILDFORD.

## *Motor Cars, Motor Cycles, & Cycles by the Best Makers.*

*Sole District Agent for*

Argyll Cars. Quadrant, Kerry, and Humber Motor Cycles.
Sunbeam, Humber, Lea Francis, and other Cycles.

OFFICIAL REPAIRER TO
Automobile Club of Great Britain and Ireland,
West Surrey Automobile Club,
Cyclists' Touring Club.

When Shalford Meadows flooded and froze over people flocked there to go skating. It was not uncommon for young boys to wait at the entrance to the meadows hoping to earn a few pennies helping the women on with their skates.

A rather attractive wooden bridge once linked Shalford Road and the towpath of the river. When the timbers rotted it was replaced in 1934 by a metal bridge.

Early motorists are being warned of the dangers of children running out into the road from St Nicolas Infants School on the Portsmouth Road. The school opened in 1860. This view dates from about 1910.

Postcard companies would publish any view. This one of the cemetery at the Mount was issued by H. A. Young of Guildford. The sender, Will, was wishing everyone well. He said: 'Baby is getting on fine and Grandma is so fond of her. Love and kisses from Muriel and Aunty and Cousin Amy. X X X X X.'

Looking up Pilgrims' Way a decade or so before the land on either side was developed for homes. The Chantries can be seen away to the right. The half-timbered 16th-century cottage on the left was once called the Pest House, suggesting that it was where those poor souls with contagious diseases were housed. At a later date its name was changed to the old Peat House, but for many years it has been called Cyder House Cottages.

The road has been laid prior to the prestigious housing development at Warwick's Bench. A location difficult to pin point today but this is most likely where South Hill becomes Warwick's Bench Road, with Racks Close on the right.

The town's first council houses were built in Cline Road, Charlotteville, in 1906. Rents for the 18 homes were between 6s 3d (31p) and 7s (35p) per week. In 1912, 20 further homes were added.

The Addison Road post office in Charlotteville doubled up as John Pennifold's bakery and confectionery shop. Mr Pennifold's brother George, is leaning on the hand-drawn bread cart. His wife, Gertrude, is standing in the doorway. The Co-op later took over the business. Note the enamel advertising sign for Hudson's soap next to the first-floor window.

A typical corner shop with its staff wearing starched white aprons. This is Kimber's Stores on the corner of Recreation Road with Woodbridge Road. Today it is a Chinese take-away.

Hundreds of people throng North Street and Market Street on December 8, 1910, to hear the result of the poll for the Guildford division of the general election. It was the second general election that year and Guildford's Conservative MP, William Edgar Horne, was again elected. This time he received 8,463 votes beating the Liberal Party candidate, Arthur Davey, by a majority of 3,631. The crowd had begun assembling at 11am, but had to wait two hours before the result was declared from the County and Borough Halls. Nationally the Liberals won the right to govern.

Named after the Drummond family of Albury Park, the Drummond Arms in Woodbridge Road was built in 1852. This picture dates from about 1911 and shows that it was a Friary Holroyd & Healy's Brewery house. The sign on the wall advertises stabling at the back and room for cycles as well!

These ancient cottages with their irregular architecture and steps leading to their doorways once stood in Park Street. They have been gone for over 40 years, probably condemned at the time as not worthy of restoration.

A decorative arch was erected in Park Street as part of the town's celebrations to commemorate the coronation of George V on June 22, 1911. The building beyond the arch was the technical school.

Under the guidance of the town's decoration committee, many streets and buildings were decorated and illuminated. This is Bridge Street looking towards the backs of the buildings in Farnham Road.

In Guildford, the celebrations commenced with a peel of bells from St Nicolas Church at 3.30am. At 7am there was a gun salute from the Castle Keep and at 10am a service of thanksgiving at St Saviour's Church. During the day there were promenade concerts and a dinner for 360 elderly people in the County and Borough Halls. Here a crowd makes its way along the upper High Street.

Mr Arthur Bullen's Humourous Car, subtitled 'My Hobby', was one of 37 entries in the Grand Procession which was part of Guildford's coronation celebrations. Illuminated by torches and lanterns, the procession assembled at the cattle market in Woodbridge Road, where this photo was taken, and proceeded through the town.

Entry number 27 was the Congregational Guild car titled 'The sailing of the Mayflower' accompanied by 40 'Puritan men and maids'. It is seen here in North Street.

Where was Guildford's market cross? It was, in fact, a temporary feature erected as part of the coronation celebrations. It was at the junction of London Road and Epsom Road. The Odeon cinema and Prudential Buildings were later built on the site of the ivy-clad house and its grounds. The Stoughton Brass and Reed Band are seen playing here.

A public weighbridge once stood at the bottom of North Street and is seen here highly decorated for either the coronation celebrations of George V or the coming of the Royal Counties Show in 1912. Sadly, the original photograph is not dated. Note the sign for the Oyster and Stewed Eel Bar.

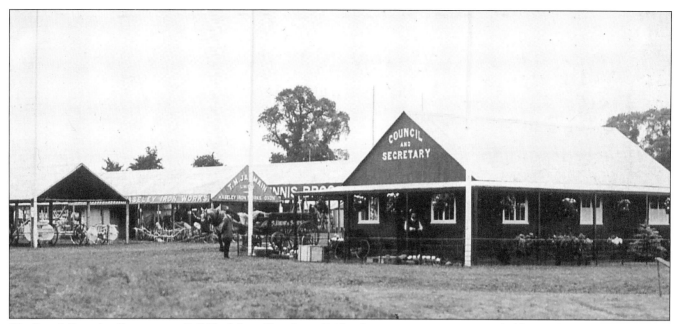

The Royal Counties Show was at Guildford from Tuesday to Friday, June 11 to 14, 1912. It was held at Stoke Hill on land that is now Bellfields Estate. There were 1,990 entries including, sheep, horses, cattle, pigs and poultry. The *Surrey Advertiser* reported: 'The show ground had been excellently laid out with displays of agricultural implements and machinery in motion.' Local tradespeople who had stands included motor manufacturers Dennis Bros; coach builders Jacobs; ironmongers Carling, Gill & Carling; tobacconists Cheel & Co; photographers Shawcross and antique furniture dealers Oliver & Sons. The show was attended by 35,518 people and there was a gospel stand which handed out 3,000 booklets courtesy of Julia (Fanny) Paynter, whose estate the show was held upon.

The town threw itself whole heartedly behind the Royal Counties Show. Streets were decorated with, as the *Surrey Advertiser* reported, 'Venetian masts linked up with festoons of pennants, while the poles themselves were clothed in red material and finished off with shields and flags.' It went on: 'The entire length of Chertsey Street and Stoke Road was decorated and both sides of the railway bridge at the foot of Nightingale Road was festooned with red, white and blue draperies, on a white ground, the intervening spaces filled with large rosettes. Above in bold letters were the words: "SUCCESS TO THE SHOW" (painted by Mr B. Snellings), the motto being flanked by an enormous flag.'

The local newspaper reported that there was a beer famine on the sweltering Thursday afternoon of the show and no doubt it was the Friary Brewery who rushed a fresh supply there. The official route from the railway station to the show was down Bridge Street and into Onslow Street, past the brewery. Here Friary erected a 40 foot high corinthian column, surmounted by the figure of a woman holding a flare. The column was draped with evergreens and palm leaves. Large signs were also put up that welcomed visitors to the town and the show.

Products once available in Guildford shops. Meat paste would have been sold in the ceramic dish marked Brett, Reynard & Co. It's High Street shop later became a restaurant called Bretts.

Shopping in the High Street. The sun shades have been drawn at White's store and note the woman on the right with her stylish perambulator.

The photographer was soon on hand to record the charred remains of W. E. White & Son's draper's store after a fire on June 24, 1914. The *Surrey Advertiser* reported that work rooms and stock rooms were gutted with thousands of pounds worth of stock damaged and that it was the most disastrous fire that had occurred in the area for some years. The fire broke out at about 4pm and it took the fire brigade well over an hour to get it under control. At one point the roof of the adjacent Lion Hotel caught alight.

White's reopened on Monday, July 20, 1914, with a huge salvage sale of its entire stock. An advertisement in the *Surrey Advertiser* proclaimed that 100 raincoats were to be offered at 1s (5p) each. Day and evening gowns were to be sold from 5s (25p) each; cotton frocks, 1s; soiled calicoes, 1d (1/2p) per yard; while sunshades and umbrellas were going for 1s (5p) each.

Stag horn hunting trophies and pot plants a plenty fill the interior of The Angel Hotel shortly after it had been bought by the Surrey Public House Trust in October 1918. Previously it had been under the ownership of a W. H. George. But its history goes back much further. The first written evidence of it being an inn is in 1527, although its undercroft dates from the 13th century.

# The 1920s, 30s and 40s

The memorial that commemorates the men from Guildford who died in World War One was unveiled in the Castle Grounds on the afternoon of Sunday, November 6, 1921. More than 5,000 people attended the service led by the Bishop of Winchester. The Mayor, Alderman G. W. Franks, and the corporation, were present along with the Guildford & District Military Band and the Salvation Army Band. Frederick Hodgson's design for the the memorial had been chosen at the end of the previous year.

The gateway into Guildford from Farnham Road with St Nicolas Church dominating the scene. On the right can be seen F. Ayres & Sons baker's shop and restaurant and on the left a selection of interesting hoardings advertising the Picture Playhouse; Ford cars, supplied by Rice Bros; and Simonds' Brewery, that hailed from Reading.

He was the baker with white hair and a beard who children thought was Santa Claus. Mr Hine ran his business from Woodbridge Road and is seen standing on the left with one of his daughters. The business remained in the family until the 1940s. Later, the shop was occupied by another well-known Guildford baker – Boyce.

By 1922, M. W. Chrismas's Victorian Dairy, occupied number 11 Chertsey Street. A decade before it had been M. Talman's Victoria Dairy. However, by 1926, Marshalls Boot Repairers occupied the site. A pair of highly polished milk churns are in the dairy cart.

Much has changed in this view of Millmead. The cottages directly in front have gone to make way for the entrance to the borough council offices. Those on the right have made way for the entrance to the Guildford Baptist Church.

Millmead looking towards St Mary's Church. The town mill is prominent and the buildings in front of it were once the iron foundry. They were demolished in 1941 and in 1965 the Yvonne Arnaud Theatre was built on the site.

A very quiet Quarry Street in the late 1920s. Someone is just leaving the Kings Head public house, which at that time was served by Hodgsons' Kingston Brewery. From 1859-66 the building on the opposite corner of the junction with Castle Street was the Guildford Dispensary – the forerunner of the Royal Surrey County Hospital.

Pimm, Son & Company was a well-known Guildford firm that employed a large number of people in its furniture shop, removals and warehouse business, its workshop and funeral department. William Pimm started the company in 1835 and within a few years had opened a shop in the High Street. However, the firm is best associated with a group of buildings in North Street opposite the Cloth Hall which it occupied from the latter half of the 19th century until 1960, when it amalgamated with a Leatherhead firm and moved to premises in the upper High Street. William Pimm's son and grandson both succeeded him in running the business. A Mr W. H. Bateman was also a director from 1916 to 1934. Here we see a staff outing to the British Empire Exhibition at Wembley Stadium in 1924.

The River Wey burst its banks on the night of Friday, January 2, 1925, and rose 5ft flooding part of the town. The town bridge was a useful vantage point.

Viewed from the iron footbridge at Millmead, the cottages here are surrounded by the floodwaters. The Mayor, J. B. Rapkins, arranged for 5cwt of coal to be delivered to each of the flooded houses so that they had plenty of dry fuel to burn.

Further along Millmead and the residents looking out of a first-floor window are smiling even if only for the photographer who, like the man in the street, must be up to his shins in water.

As good a place as any to stand and view the floods! The lorry is parked in the iron foundry works.

Paddock Gardens, by Shalford Meadows, looks a wash-out. The *Surrey Times* reported that nearby at least two huge elm trees were blown down.

No boats or teas today! A stranded Allen's boat house seen here from Quarry Street. Within two days the flood waters had subsided.

Normal service has been resumed! Allen's Boathouse and River Lounge – the perfect place to spend a lazy summer's afternoon.

Rosemary Alley has probably looked much the same for a couple of hundred years. How many feet have trod those well worn steps from Millbrook to Quarry Street?

A number of narrow passages once led into the High Street. Milkhouse Gate is an example which remains, but this is Smallpeice's Gateway. It was situated between the Playhouse Arcade and Tunsgate.

Mums natter while children play in South Street, now part of Sydenham Road. The site is currently being redeveloped for a new multi-storey car park. The tile-hung building was once a public house called the Queens Head.

The motor manufacturers Dennis Bros are well known for their fire engines, buses and lorries. In fact, they could turn their hand to vehicles of any description as the one here testifies. Presumably an advertising gimmick for Capt. Andy Hawks' Show Boat Floating Theatre, the signwriting suggests that it was bound for Brighton. It is seen here at the bottom of Woodbridge Hill, near the Dennis factory, in the late 1920s.

The borough council's housing estate at Westborough was largely built in the 1920s. The safeguard bus travelling along Southway is passing Fairfield Rise. The sign beside the road reads: 'WARNING TO PEDESTRIANS TAR SPRAYING IN PROGRESS'.

The lens used to take this picture has compressed the view making it hard to identify. The photographer was standing on The Mount, looking northwards. In the foreground is Mount Farm. One building that can be identified in the middle foreground is today's Crawford House Hotel, on the Farnham Road.

The Guildford division of St John Ambulance was formed in 1890 by 26 men who were members of a Bible studies group. Led by Martin Williamson, a member of a Guildford family which ran a successful furniture store, these volunteers soon acquired a horse-drawn ambulance. They were kept busy transporting patients to nearby hospitals under the direction of local doctors. By 1927 the division was based in Woodbridge Road with its garage in Leas Road. It had three motor ambulances one of which is seen here with its first full-time paid ambulance man, Bert Farler.

The Lido was opened in 1933 and the Borough of Guildford corps of St John Ambulance, as it was then known, set up a first-aid post in the grounds. It stood on the north side and had a poolside and a roadside entrance.

When Dennis Bros vacated their factory on the corner of Bridge Street and Onslow Street a number of other businesses moved in, including the Rodboro Boot & Shoe Company. Another firm who had a shop there was Quittenton's. It moved from the High Street in 1930 when Maurice Quittenton Jnr, with the help of his elder sister, took over from his father. In 1934 the business moved to Tunsgate where it remained until it ceased trading in 1964.

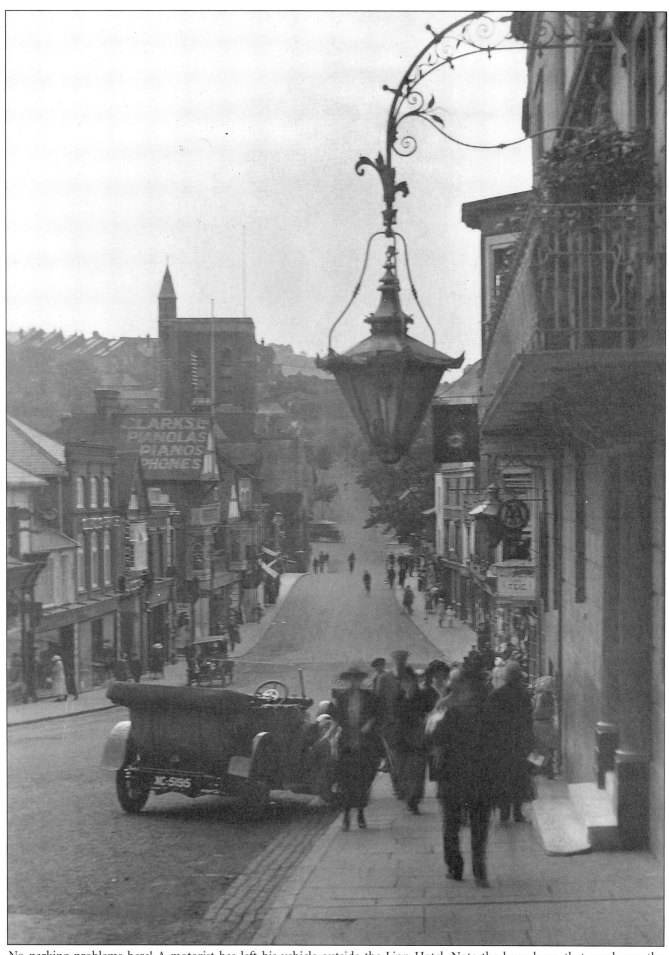

No parking problems here! A motorist has left his vehicle outside the Lion Hotel. Note the huge lamp that overhangs the pavement. Also, Clarks Piano Shop was not shy when it came to advertising its business! Would you be allowed to paint a huge sign on your roof today?

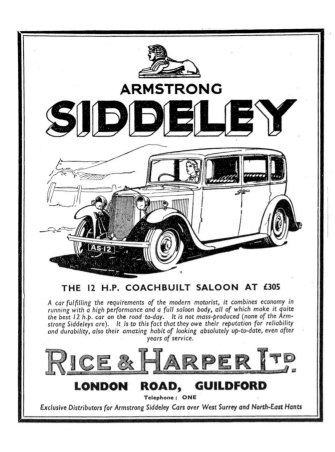

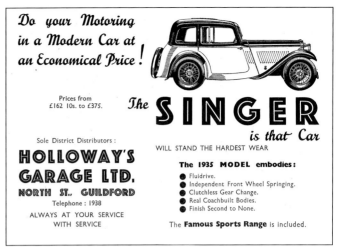

Advertisements from the *Guildford City Outlook* magazine of 1935.

Going underground: Many years ago there were guided tours of the caverns at Racks Close. The tunnels were dug for chalk during Medieval times but today are considered too dangerous for the public to visit. In 1984 a lorry crashed into Castle Arch damaging the 13th-century structure and the caverns were reopened for replacement materials known as chalk clunch.

This little shop at 39 Quarry Street had a number of occupants during the first half of the 20th century. The 1910 town directory lists the occupant as an F. Stickley; six years later it is a general shop with a W. Cook as resident. An F. Smith was there in about 1922, while the 1925 directory gives the name H. Stephens, suggesting a possible date for this photograph. By 1930 it had become The Tearooms only to change its name by 1936 to the Cavern Tearooms, no doubt after the nearby Racks Close caverns.

According to the signs of the Good Intent Apartment House in Quarry Street, accommodation was available to men only. Next door, at The Cavern tearooms, Woodbines and other brands of 'smokes' could be bought.

Guildford's locomotive shed and turntable in the pre-war days of the Southern Railway. The siding in which the train waits was at one time used to store a breakdown train with its large red crane. Note the signal box near the entrance to the chalk tunnel.

Several fine motor vehicles are seen in this view of the High Street at its junction with Quarry Street. Note the policeman on point duty who has just waved the cyclists through. Also, with the exception of about three, all the vehicles are painted in very dark colours. Shades of Henry Ford's well known comment: 'Any colour you like as long as it's black'.

An "N" class Southern Railway locomotive pulls out of Guildford station with a mixed train including a horse box and a flat wagon containing a Co-op Wholesale Society road tanker. The electric third rail, which can be seen, was laid by July 1937.

Onslow Village was built in the early 1920s when in response to a housing shortage Lord Onslow sold land at Manor and Wilderness Farms for a knock down price of £57 per acre. A public utility society was formed with the borough council who loaned £20,000 to the scheme. The management committee of Onslow Village met for the first time on March 20, 1920, at the offices of Colonel W. J. Perkins, solicitor, 133 High Street, Guildford. A foundation stone was laid by the Countess of Onslow on May 1, 1920, and within two months the first homes were completed. This 1930s view was taken from the Hog's Back and two cheeky schoolboys are posing for the camera.

Litchfield Way, Onslow Village, before the beech hedges were planted. It is named after Frederick Litchfield who was the proposed chairman of the management committee. It is unlikely that he ever took up his position as in 1921 he helped create a similar project in Cape Town, South Africa, returning after two years to his home in Hampstead where shortly after he died.

About 600 homes were built in Onslow Village. However, some of the original drawings show that there were plans to develop further, across the farmland to the north of the A3. By the mid 1970s, one third of the properties were still owned by Onslow Village Ltd. Then, in 1984, the company was wound up and many shareholders and tenants had the chance to buy their homes at extremely affordable prices. The picture shows Manor Way in the 1930s.

The 1930s witnessed something of a house-building boom in the borough. The population rose from just under 40,000 in 1933, to nearly 50,000 by 1941. Estates such as Dennisville at Guildford Park (1934) and much ribbon development took place, as seen here in Worplesdon Road, Stoughton.

The advertisements seen here, from the *Guildford City Outlook* magazine of 1934, show that a new semi-detached home cost from £675 freehold. These characteristic houses, with their bay windows, came with tiled bathrooms and chrome fittings – the very latest in 1930s luxury. Homes at the Winterhill Estate in Burpham were more expensive, but, as the advertisement claimed, had been 'designed by an eminent architect to suit individual plots and to catch maximum sunlight'.

Leonard Barrow on his milk round for the Lymposs & Smee Dairy in the 1920s. Richard Lymposs started out as a dairyman in Guildford in 1820. He kept 20 cows in a yard off what is now the upper High Street and grazed them in fields near Foxenden Quarry and where Lower Edgeborough Road/Clandon Road is today. In 1860 the business transferred to 173 High Street and later to premises in Sydenham Road. Sons and grandsons carried on the business and in 1920 it amalgamated with a Mr Smee's dairy, in Friary Street.

The dairy cart has become larger and now Mr Barrow has a horse to pull it along. The date is 1935 and he would have made two deliveries per day – the first delivering fresh milk at breakfast time and later, the main delivery. Note the thermos-type flask on the top of the cart that was filled with ice cream.

Believed to be in the Sydenham Road area, a fully loaded Lymposs & Smee milk float with the old wide-mouth bottles that were sealed with a cardboard disc.

Advertisement from the *Guildford City Outlook* magazine of 1935.

An advertisement in the local press said it all: 'Good news says J. E. Jackson, the Studebaker Miracle Convoy will visit Guildford next Tuesday and Wednesday, April 16 and 17, 1935'. And so it did; the cavalcade of vehicles seen here are behind Jackson's Garage at the bottom of the High Street. Experts from the Studebaker company were on hand to give advice and no doubt tried to make a few sales. Prices started from £298. The 'miracle' part of the event was that one of the cars was tilted to an angle of 58 degrees demonstrating its low centre of gravity. The miniature car was a replica of the manufacturer's Roadster model.

Crowds gathered at the Josephs Road football ground for an open-air service of thanks giving to mark the silver jubilee of King George V on May 6, 1935. Pictured on the stage are the Mayor and Mayoress, Alderman W. G. L. Sheppard and his wife; the Deputy Mayor and Deputy mayoress, Alderman William Harvey and his wife; and in the centre the Archdeacon of Surrey, the Ven L. E. Blackburne.

During silver jubilee day there were a number of events in the town which included the opening of the Stoke Park rock gardens and the yachting and boating pools, a carnival procession, folk dancing and an ABA boxing tournament. Later that evening there were fireworks and a huge bonfire on Pewley Hill. This is the mock castle entrance at the bottom of the High Street. The following views show the town decorated for the event.

Plenty of flags and bunting in Friary Street.

The entrance to Jackson's Garage is on the right and the Lion Hotel can be seen on the left. Just below it are the offices of Clarke, Gammon & Emerys, estate agents.

Note how the street lamps were strung across the High Street and that Marks & Spencer was where Boots is today.

At the top of the High Street, by Abbot's Hospital, another arch, covered in greenery, was erected. It contained a large number of paper roses made by a group of women at the drill hall in Sandfield Terrace.

The art-deco style Odeon Cinema was opened on May 13, 1935, by the Mayor, Alderman W. G. L. Sheppard. The first film shown was *Brewster's Millions* starring Jack Buchanan. He sent a telegram wishing the Odeon well. The *Surrey Advertiser* reported that before the performance musical selections were provided by Alan Parsons and his orchestra.

Guildford celebrities of the 1930s caricatured by Matt and published in the Sunday Graphic.

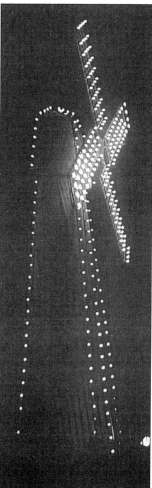

Five views of the town specially lit to mark the coronation of George VI on May 12, 1937. The unmistakable Guildhall; an arch of lights along Market Street seen from the High Street; the rockery in the Jubilee Gardens at Stoke Park; a mock windmill with rotating sails at Mount Farm; the High Street and Holy Trinity Church draped in long red and green banners with gold crowns.

Tyler & Co Ltd's off licence at 40 High Street, with flags flying at about the time of the 1937 coronation. The company was formed in Woking in 1902 and by the time it was taken over by the Victoria Wine Company in 1965, there were 163 shops in and around Surrey. Tyler's was linked to the Friary Brewery and sold its Golden Eagle Brand whisky, which is being advertised in the shop window. It had another shop in the upper High Street that sold a wider range of provisions.

Water jugs advertising the Friary Brewery's Golden Eagle Brand whisky.

The latest 1930s fashions were available from one of the town's premiere stores, W. E. White & Son.

Advertisement from the *Guildford City Outlook* magazine of 1935. Fund raising was as important then as it is today.

Edgar Purnell established his mineral water manufacturing business in Guildford in 1918. During the 1920s and 1930s he became one of the town's best known tradesmen and was president of the Chamber of Trade in 1927-28. After he died in 1936 his family continued the business until 1952 when it was taken over by the Sussex firm Fryco. Purnell & Co Ltd was one of the last companies in the UK to sell ginger beer in stoneware bottles, which it did until the late 1940s.

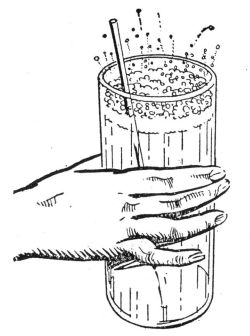

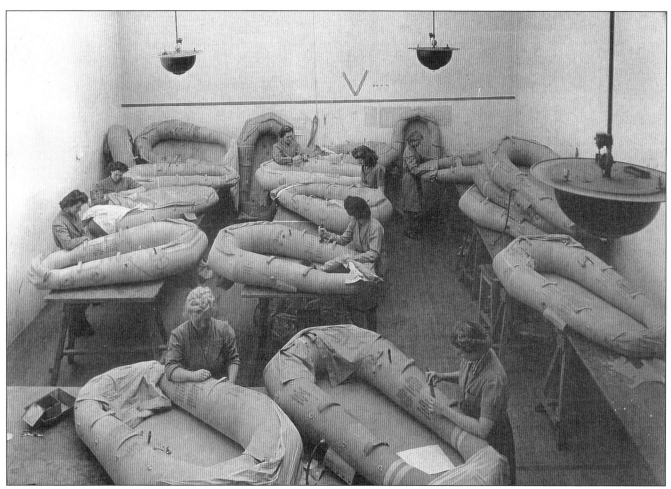

Women played a vital role in industry during World War Two. RFD, a company formed by Reginald Foster Dagnell, produced life-rafts and flotation bags for aircraft at its Stoke Road factory. It expanded into premises at Godalming and also took over a sports hall in Cross Lanes (pictured) where dinghies were assembled.

Although the women at RFD worked long hours, they still managed to find time for recreation. They formed a ladies football team seen here having won two trophies during the 1942 season.

Men of the 4th (Guildford) Battalion Surrey Home Guard on parade in Shalford Park. Formed as the Local Defence Volunteers (LDV) in May 1940, they were commanded by Col Guy Westland Geddes who had retired to Guildford in 1934 after 34 years of military service.

At its Woodbridge factory Dennis Bros helped the war effort by manufacturing tanks, armoured vehicles, trailer pumps, lorries, small parts for aircraft and even bombs. The workforce rose to 3,000 during the war. Seen here are the engineering apprentices in June 1944. Sitting in the front row in the centre are, from left, the works manager, Mr Halpike; the managing director, Cecil T. Skipper; and the foreman to the apprentices, Mr Denham. This is a companion photograph to that of the trade apprentices featured on page 127 in the author's previous book, *Guildford The War Years – 1939-45*, co-written with Graham Collyer.

There have only been two Anglican cathedrals in the UK built on entirely new sites since Medieval times – Liverpool and Guildford. The foundation stone for Guildford Cathedral was laid by the Archbishop of Canterbury, Dr Cosmo Gordon Lang, in 1936. Building work was halted during World War Two and did not begin again until 1952, following a determined fund-raising campaign. The Cathedral of the Holy Spirit was consecrated by Bishop Reindorp on May 17, 1961, in the presence of the Queen and the Duke of Edinburgh. This aerial view dates from 1946.

The afternoon sunlight picks out the town's best known landmark, the Guildhall clock. The clock's casing dates from 1683 when the front of the Guildhall was rebuilt. Its mechanism, which is actually inside the building, is thought to date from about 1561. It was made by John Aylward who donated it to the town in return for being allowed to set up in business here.

# The 1950s and 60s

The ladieswear department of W. E. White & Sons' store in its closing years. This prestigious shop had two fronts – the main entrance on the High Street, its windows displaying ladies fashions, while the North Street entrance was dedicated to menswear. Some of the staff lived in and although all the staff had the usual paid holidays, White's generously gave them an extra three days each spring after the rigours of the winter sale.

Lingerie and children's wear neatly displayed at White's, where an older-style of service was offered. Staff were trained to serve the customer no matter what the inconvenience. Each department had its own buyer. The buyer would be courted by a medley of commercial travellers and were received in the importance of their company's standing. The rest of the sales staff were graded down to the junior who was mostly a servant to the others. Marks & Spencer bought out White's in the early 1960s ending the life of an emporium that had served the town since 1877.

Workmen in the High Street outside the Three Pigeons public house appear to be replacing some of Guildford's famous granite setts. Borough surveyor Henry Peak introduced this type of road surface to the town in 1868. The setts are sometimes incorrectly referred to as cobble stones.

Masseys was a well known chemist's shop that stood on the corner of Chertsey Street and the upper High Street. A few doors up was a building that housed the town's art gallery, which many years before had been Joseph Whittaker Barfoot's Paperhanging Warehouse. This enterprising businessman founded the *Surrey Advertiser* in 1864.

The old Baptist Chapel in Castle Square, with, to the right, Tunsgate leading to the High Street. The chapel was built in 1860 and a number of alterations were made in 1874. It was demolished in 1954.

An interior view of the Baptist Chapel and its cumbersome but rather splendid heating system!

Today there are Lincolnshire and Cumberland but once there were Taplins Guildford Sausages – the name of a pork butcher who traded in Chertsey Street.

Decorating paints, varnishes and distempers were sold by Daisy Ranger at her Chertsey Street shop. This building has now been absorbed by the adjoining Spread Eagle public house.

One for the bus enthusiasts to drool over! Passing the Prince of Wales public house in Woodbridge Road, are from left, a Yellow Bus Services (YBS) Bedford Utility bus, a YBS Dennis Lancet J3 and a Safeguard Dennis Lancet 1.

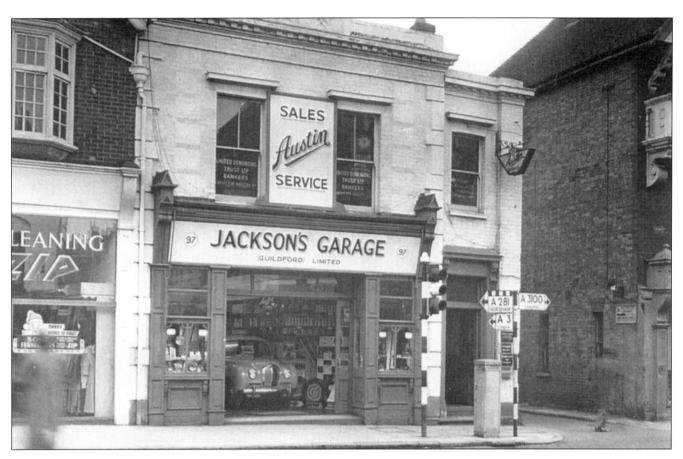

Jackson's Garage, at the bottom of the High Street (number 97) opposite Friary Street, was an Austin dealership for many years. By the late 1950s Zip Cleaners occupied number 97a, while to the other side of the garage was Courts furnishing store.

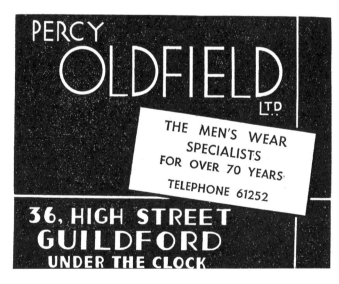

Three local advertisements from *Kelly's Directory of Guildford, Godalming and Neighbourhood, 1959.*

The Lion Hotel during its final days in the 1950s. It was not long before the demolition team moved in and by the end of that decade an F. W. Woolworth store stood in its place.

Many people will remember the cafeteria, roof gardens and fish ponds on the top of Harvey's store.

On a sunny afternoon two women contemplate the stepping stones in the roof garden of Harvey's.

Friary Square in the 1950s. The corrugated iron hut was where the Guildford company Plastic Coatings Ltd was founded by Nigel Vinson. With a staff of four the firm began by coating domestic items such as draining racks. It soon expanded and in 1956 moved to its present site at Woodbridge Meadows. Further factories were opened in Cheshire, Leicestershire and Gwent, but for many years Plastic Coatings has been under different ownership. The man on the extreme left is about to walk over the tubular steel footbridge that led to the Farnham Road bus station.

Harvey's Arcade in the 1950s. William Harvey set up his outfitters business in 1919. By the early 1920s it was situated within the Picture Playhouse Arcade. The firm transferred across the road in 1948. Known as the Army & Navy store in recent years, it closed early in 2000 for a major refit and will reopen as House of Fraser.

There were two flights of steep steps from the road level in Quarry Street down to the front doors of these cottages. Today this area is landscaped and looks out on to Millbrook.

The Castle Grounds are a perfect place to spend a summer's afternoon. Here the 12th-century keep looks down over the bowling green and the memorial to the men from Guildford who fell during World War One. The chimney of the old swimming baths in Castle Street can be seen.

Candy Corner, a sweet shop and tobacconists, no less, was on the corner of Tunsgate and South Street. It is seen here from the entrance of the Castle Grounds shortly before it was demolished in the 1950s.

A view of Castle Square with the entrance to the Castle Grounds on the right. At the end of the 1950s Miss G. Robinson and Mrs M. Tindall were the proprietors of The Joke Shop. These premises later became the Castle Buttery restaurant which is now the Peking Garden restaurant.

An interesting mixture of 1950s posters on the wall of Candy Corner featuring the H-bomb and the Civil Defence, Premium Bonds, and the Guildford Cinema.

South Street, now Sydenham Road, circa 1950. Beyond the three pedestrians is Oxford Terrace and further along was Jessie Bullen's sweet shop.

Stevens' Fish and Chip Shop and Hope's newsagents in South Street, now Sydenham Road. The shop next door was a boot repairers. The advertisement for *Woman* magazine boasts that it is illustrated in glorious full colour.

Sydenham Road and the same pedestrians as the previous two pictures. The sign in the centre of the picture is above the gateway to J. Franks, Building Contractors, Decorators and Sanitary Engineers. The Jehovah's Witness meeting room is next door.

The town's post-war carnivals were popular with local companies as well as groups and societies who loved having a float and dressing up for the occasion. These are members of the Guildford Youth Groups in the early 1950s.

Cycle speedway was a post-war sport which captured the imagination of many teenage boys. The South West Surrey League was fiercely contested and included the Guildford Aces, Stoughton Stars, Dennisville Rockets, Guildford Greyhounds, and the Westway Bluebirds. Another team, the Guildford Park Panthers, are pictured here.

Part of the fun of cycle speedway was constructing the bicycles from whatever was available – old frames, peddles, cranks and particularly wheels, as these were frequently kicked in by opponents. You could spot the homes where the fanatics lived as there were always freshly painted parts strung from the washing line. Safety helmets were often home-made out of papier mache hardened with several coats of paint. Here are members of the Guildford Aces and Stoughton Stars at the Station Meadows.

The Guildford Aces were formed with the help of Eric Read, the Commanding Officer of the Guildford Sea Cadets and George Gaff, whose two sons, Patrick and Andrew, were keen to race competitively. The borough allowed the team to construct a track at Station Meadows, now the Post Office sorting depot in Walnut Tree Close.

Large crowds came to watch the Guildford Aces when they raced on Saturday afternoons. They switched to Saturday evenings after a director of Guildford City Football Club wrote saying that they were taking away many of their fans! George Gaff pulled off something of a coup when on April 21, 1951, he persuaded the well-known broadcaster Brian Johnston to come to Guildford for the opening of the Aces' new track. 'Johnners' rode around the track giving a live commentary for the In Town To-night radio programme. He is seen here talking to Eric Read.

Within a few years the heyday of cycle speedway was over. Its demise can be linked to the fact that many of the boys had grown up and were doing their National Service, or had moved on to riding motor-cycles. Also, the cycle manufacturers were trying to cash in and were offering ready-to-ride bikes. Unfortunately, this took the fun out of building those home-made machines.

The Aldershot & District Traction Company ran its first bus services into Guildford via Ash and Pirbright in 1914. The 1920s saw much competition between rival bus companies with the A&D coming out on top in many instances in what has been described as the Bus Wars. A garage was opened in Onslow Street, but the company soon outgrew it, moving to new premises in Woodbridge Road in 1927. This garage was periodically expanded until 1958. The company became a subsidiary of the National Bus Company in 1969 and Thames Valley buses in 1972. The once familiar green buses were repainted maroon with the fleet name Alder Valley and the NBC logo painted on their sides.

A Dennis Lancet J3 bus of the Safeguard Company passing some of the post-war prefabricated housing in Westborough during the 1950s. The company's origins go back to 1924 when Arthur Newman, who ran a coal delivery business from Guildford Park, had a charabanc body fitted to the chassis of a lorry.

On route from Westborough to Guildford, a Bedford Duple, owned by the Safeguard Bus Company, passes Avenue Terrace in Woodbridge Road in the late 1950s. Within a few years these houses had been pulled down.

Hammond & Sons owned three buses that ran between Guildford and Wonersh. This one was made by Dennis and has stopped in Quarry Street outside Guildford Museum to pick up passengers. By the early 1950s Hammond's buses were nearly at the end of their working lives and soon after the company ceased to operate.

Train spotters standing on platform 8 in the days of steam would have had a good view of locomotives passing through the coaling stage. The loco in the foreground is of the S15 class, introduced in 1920 for either freight or passenger trains.

Within a few years of this late 1950s view the end of steam was looming and the remaining locomotives soon became very run-down and dirty. British Railways found it hard to employ cleaners within its depots, traditionally a low-paid job. Note the piles of ash and clinker mounting up by the lineside.

New potatoes at 3d (1.25p) per pound and English tomatoes selling for 1s 4d (6.6p) per pound are some of the special offers at the Madrid Road branch of the Guildford Co-operative Society in Guildford Park. Judging by the other produce in the windows it was an extremely well stocked mini market.

Read all about it! The world's news comes to Surrey's county town. Gone are the days when vendors stood on the streets of Guildford selling national newspapers, as seen here on the corner of the High Street and Market Street in the 1960s. However, nowadays you do have the chance to buy a copy of *The Big Issue*, the revenue from which helps the homeless.

Fire ripped through the Royal Grammar School on Sunday, December 2, 1962, destroying part of the top floor and main staircase. The alarm was raised at 6.53am and six fire appliances attended. The only person injured was Mr R. W. Smoothey, the art master, who was hit on the head by a falling lampshade as he was trying to salvage items from the burning building.

These picture were taken soon after the fire had been put out. Holes in the roof can clearly be seen. Note also the rather spartan Christmas decorations strung across the upper High Street.

The fire was believed to have been caused by an electrical fault in the the east wing. The water used to put out the blaze saturated much of the building's timbers and afterwards dry rot set in. While rebuilding, the workmen who exposed the oak lintels over the windows found them riddled with death watch beetle. However, expert restoration work was completed under the instructions of the architect David Nye. The limewash finish was criticised, but Mr Nye defended it saying that buildings looked like this in early times.

The Dolphin was a Courage public house on the corner of North Street and Chertsey Street where the American theme restaurant TGI Friday's is today. This was the second Dolphin public house built on or about this site. It lasted from 1915 to 1964.

North Street in 1962 showing the then relatively new library. Traders here at about this time included boot repairers Sharp & Dunwell, Bernards the grocers, and beyond the library, Mac's Milk Bar, which later became the Silver Star Restaurant.

The Royal Arms Commercial Hotel and Restaurant in North Street with the adjoining Guildford Institute in Ward Street. By the time this photo was taken in the early 1960s the hotel and restaurant had closed and later re-opened as a bank.

Henry Peak's building that for many years was the Surrey Arms public house still stands in North Street on the corner of Haydon Place. Before it became a pizza restaurant in the mid 1980s it had been run by several different breweries including Richard Elkins' North Street Brewery, Hodgsons' of Kingston and finally, Courage.

Tucked away in North Place, the Live and Let Live is a small public house that survives today. However, the buildings to the left and right of it have all gone.

Market Street at the junction with North Street and a whole host of shops which are no longer trading. On the right was Lavells confectioners and newsagents, next door a Wimpey bar, further up Sandra Shoes, then Osbornes' stores. Gammons the drapers and outfitters, who also sold home furnishings, once dominated the opposite side. Further up was Coles' radio shop and Mac Fisheries.

Sunlight picks out the decorative feature on the Co-operative building in North Street. The Guildford & District Co-operative Society was formed in 1891 with its registered office in Haydon Place. In 1935 a dairy was established. The Guildford Society operated in an area surrounding the town as far as Leatherhead and Dorking and even into parts of West Sussex. It merged with the Royal Arsenal Co-operative Society in 1971, at which time it had 42,000 members and 350 employees.

Co-operative corner with Leapale Road and the Congregational Church. This picture dates from circa 1963, when the Co-op was a major store in Guildford.

There have been many changes to the town since this photo was taken in the early 1960s. It shows the then unfinished cathedral, the Methodist Church (bottom left) and the Friary Brewery to the right. The Woodbridge Press building in Onslow Street, now Bar Mambo, can just be seen. The cinema in Woodbridge Road, now Bojanglez nightclub, was then called the Astor. It seems the only business pictured here that survives today is the outfitters Moffat & Co, founded in 1927.

A row of shops in Onslow Street approximately where the taxi rank outside the Friary shopping centre is today.

Part of the former militia barracks that was home to various businesses before it was demolished. Here, in the part that was Onslow Street, we see Buyers, the second-hand shop; Ayres bakers; while out of view to the right was Coombs motor dealers. On the first floor was the Alby John School of Dancing. Fogwills Ltd, was in Friary Street and their seeds were sent to all parts of the world.

A rare view from inside Friary Square. The dance school can be seen and to the right there had once been a row of cottages.

Take a walk down Friary Street today and still discernible is the building that was once the Bear public house. It is seen here in its final years when it served Courage ales. The building's origins go back to the 16th century.

The gardens at the back of these properties in Quarry Street once ran down to a millstream. Part of the gardens were lost when Millbrook was constructed to ease the town's traffic congestion.

Many will remember the big freeze of 1962-63 when this photograph of Shalford Meadows was taken. The winter of 1895 had also been a particularly harsh one, as had 1947.

An icy cold Millmead during the winter of 1963. The open space to the right of the river, in the middle foreground, would soon become home to the Debenhams store, named Plummers when it first opened.

The framework for Plummers store in Millbrook is seen here taking shape in the mid-1960s. Its basement and ground floor was flooded in September 1968. It was renamed Debenhams in December 1972.

The crew of the class 2 tank locomotive fill it with water before coupling it up to its carriages further down the platform and departing for Horsham via Cranleigh. These locos provided much of the motive power for this branch line during its final years. Closed as part of the Beeching Plan, regular service ceased on June 12, 1965, although a special excursion train ran the following day.

Southern Region railway station signs of the 1950s/60s.

Battle of Britain class loco No. 34082, 615 Squadron, drifts into Guildford a couple of years before the end of steam on the Southern Region in 1967. Although this engine was cut up for scrap, its 'sister' loco No. 34081, 92 Squadron, was preserved along with several hundred other locos. Many are in steam once again on heritage railways, while one or two can be seen hauling 'steam specials' on the main line.

Nicknamed Nelsons, because of their one-eyed appearance and the fact that they worked the Waterloo to Portsmouth line, these electric trains were a common sight passing through Guildford from the late 1930s to the 1970s. An example has been preserved at the National Railway Museum in York.

During the summer of 1967 Guildford's semi-roundhouse engine shed with its turntable was a place of pilgrimage for train spotters witnessing the final months of southern steam. A few managed to sneak past the shed master to have a rare look inside. Artist David Shepherd got to know the staff there well and was allowed unlimited access. After a day in his studio at Hascombe painting his famous wildlife pictures he would drive to Guildford's loco shed. He has described it as being 'loaded with coal dust and lovely steam-engine smoke'. Time was running out, often he could only stay a while making the briefest of sketches of those other 'beautiful' giants.

Up until 1966 an ambulance service in south-west Surrey was provided by the Guildford corps of St John Ambulance. When it was taken over by Surrey County Council it had 20 full-time ambulancemen plus a manager and three control staff. This is the fleet outside the Leas Road Depot shortly before the hand-over.

Work is taking place to create a new room to the foyer of St Saviour's Church hall in Leas Road. The hall was built in 1960, replacing an older hall that stood almost opposite St Saviour's at the old junction of Woodbridge Road and Onslow Street. St Saviour's opened a new church centre in 1993, making the Leas Road hall redundant. It was sold that year for demolition.

For many years The Bellows antique shop was at 78 Woodbridge Road on the corner with Church Road. Resembling something of an 'old curiosity shop' full to the rafters with all manner of collectables it certainly caught the eye of an American visitor to the town. The story goes that he was so taken by what he saw, that he bought every item in the shop and shipped them back home!

Guildford's cattle market was in Woodbridge Road from 1896 to 1969. It is seen here in its closing years before it moved to Slyfield. This market closed in 2000 ending a tradition in the town that went back more than 700 years.

Hills was a furniture store that occupied a building in Onslow Street that had once been a house. In 1904 it was extended and turned into a shop by Charles Sutton who traded as Chas Sutton & Co, selling ladies and gents clothing, boots, shoes and general drapery. The house had been owned by his mother-in-law, Mrs Miles, and for the previous 10 years or so he had traded from two small shops on the opposite side of Onslow Street. The business was carried on by the Sutton family until the early 1950s when Hills became tenants. The part at the far end was let to the National Business Agency, then to Safeguard Coaches Ltd, as their booking office and finally to a chiropodist. It was pulled down in 1974 after compulsory purchase.

Many readers will have vivid memories of the September 1968 floods. Rain fell heavily on the Saturday night of the 14th and the following day. On the Monday the River Wey burst its banks and flooded the town. The author – then eight years old – had his first glimpse of the floods here at Ladymead on the Monday afternoon, at about the same time as these pictures were taken.

Children soon realised that the flood waters provided a great source of entertainment. It was better than the seaside! Employees from the Aldershot & District bus garage watch from the first floor as a dinghy full of excited passengers goes by.

Shop owners did not view the floods in quite the same light. Here at the bottom of the High Street it has ruined much of their stock. There was plenty of mopping up to do once the waters subsided.

The flood water has dropped but there are plenty of sightseers while businesses try to get back to work.

This Safeguard bus ploughs through the 1968 flood waters in front of Grays Garage in Woodbridge Meadows. Look at the names of the motor manufacturers on the front of the building. Are any still in business?

Two-way traffic in Bridge Street and a policeman on point duty as well! The Aldershot & District double decker bus is making its way past the Railway Hotel towards the Farnham Road bus station.

By the early 1960s the Battersea College of Advanced Technology had outgrown its London premises and was looking for a new home. Guildford had been considering the idea of creating a university and an agreement was made for the college to relocate here. Building work at Stag Hill started in January 1966 and the university was officially opened within two years.

The concept of the University of Surrey was to create a new community – a town within a town on a hill. Stag Hill, in the shadow of the cathedral, was the obvious site unlike other town's whose post-war universities were created some two or three miles out. It was deemed close enough to the town centre to allow the university and its inhabitants to integrate with other aspects of life in and around Guildford.

To many Guildfordians the building of the university was a huge project. However, looking back some 30 years to these photos and comparing them to its expansion in recent years, the original development appears quite small.

# *The 1970s and 80s*

Friary Street before it was redeveloped and pedestrianised. At about this time petrol was sold by Court & Smith motor dealers; there was Peter Dominic wine merchants; Perfect Cleaners and a host of other businesses including Hardy's outfitters and pawnbrokers, Tuson & Sons.

Much change is taking place around the old treadmill crane building beside the river. What was the Bear public house in Friary Street, seen here on the left, is now retail premises.

Dapdune Crescent in Woodbridge Road just prior to demolition. Years before these had been prestigious family homes. In their final years the occupants included the YMCA hostel at number 3, Williamson & Sons antique dealer's at number 4, Guildford Crusaders Hall at number 5, and at number 6, Dr Whitaker's surgery.

Farewell to the Prince of Wales. The year is 1972 and the Woodbridge Road public house, next to St Saviour's Church, is being stripped of its tiles ready for demolition.

When the Methodist Church on the corner of Woodbridge Road and North Street was demolished in 1973 it would appear that part of it came down quicker than was planned. A policeman and two men – possibly workmen – survey the fallen masonry.

The old Friary Brewery buildings succumb to the ball and chain to make way for the Friary shopping centre.

A rather tatty row of buildings in Onslow Street not long before they were demolished. John Sutton, who took this photograph, reminded the author of a well-known character who once lived thereabouts. His name was 'Choppy" Ayling and on Saturday nights he sold seafood from a barrow outside the Vintners Arms in North Street. On Sundays he went around the streets selling cockles, mussels and winkles.

Sign writing from days gone by above Heathorns Turf Accountants in Onslow Street, photographed shortly before demolition in the 1970s.

The Seven Stars public house in Swan Lane in 1973. A year later it was bombed by the IRA along with the Horse and Groom public house in North Street. Five people lost their lives at the latter of the two pubs. Both re-opened, but the Seven Stars soon closed and reopened as an off licence.

Onslow Street in May 1973 and the premises of two well-known Guildford firms are being demolished. To the left is the builders' yard of Tribe & Robinson and next to it Bowden & Higlett's Onslow Electrical Works. The new police station can be seen in the background.

It is said that Asian cuisine is now Britain's favourite restaurant food. Until recent years, however, there were relatively few Indian restaurants in Guildford. This is a rare picture of the Shahee Mahal in October 1975 when it was at 4 Commercial Road. A local newspaper advertisement for the restaurant in December 1974 stated that it specialised in Indian, Chinese and Continental food. There was seating for 60 people, discounts for students, and it would be open on both Christmas Day and Boxing Day.

Guildford's Pilgrim Morris Men outside the Cannon public house in Portsmouth Road. Once part of the adjacent Cannon Brewery, it was for many years a Friary pub. In 1973 part of it was turned into a wine bar called the Battery Vault Cellar Bar. Trends come and go and in 2000 it had another facelift and now goes by the name of The Power House.

The Carpenters Arms in Leapale Road was around 100 years old when a fire broke out on Easter Sunday 1976. The pub's tenant was George Digby. His wife Dolly, 73, was overcome by smoke and lay unconscious on the top floor of the three-storey building. The *Surrey Advertiser* reported that a group of Irish tinkers who had been drinking in the pub rescued Mrs Digby and carried her to safety. The pub re-opened later that year and in 1982 was refurbished once again, re-opening as the Mary Rose.

A wet Onslow Street looking towards the Rodboro Buildings in the 1970s. The removal company Pickfords had occupied the site on the right for many years.

A snap shot of the Castle Inn, Park Street, in 1974. Built in the 1880s, it was swept away along with its adjoining off licence in 1986 to make way for a large office development.

Residents of Charlotteville nicknamed the public house in Cooper Road the Pig and Tater after the produce they grew and the livestock they kept on their allotment gardens. In 1976 its real name, the Foresters Inn (later the Foresters Arms) was finally dropped in favour of the locals' choice.

Two establishments which once had porches. Here we see Stevens' fish and chip shop and the Prince Albert public house in Stoke Road. Further along can be seen the tiny newsagents that stood at the top of Stoke Fields.

In 1975 the Guildford division of St John Ambulance moved from its Woodbridge Road premises to a new building in Stocton Close – a site formerly used by Blue Saloon coaches. The official opening of the new headquarters took place on July 13 of that year. Seen here is corps superintendent Ron Snape talking to the cadets. The division is still busy to this day providing an excellent first-aid service at events such as the Surrey County Show in Stoke Park, at Spectrum leisure centre and countless local fetes, as well as helping out at the London Marathon and giving support to the Surrey Ambulance Service.

To prevent further urbanisation the Friary Brewery bought Pewley Down in 1919 and gifted it to the town as a memorial to those who had died in World War One. This snowy view looks across the valley to the Chantries. All that remains today of the thatched roof shelter is its concrete base.

It's 1980 and behind these buildings on the corner of Commercial Road the Friary centre is taking shape. These too would soon be pulled down to make way for the entrance to the shopping centre and bus station.

With the opening of the Friary shopping centre in 1981 came a new public house – The Blackfriars. However, just over seven years later it was converted into several shop units during a revamp of the centre.

The Little White Lion public house in North Street closed at about the time the White Lion Walk shopping mall was being developed in the mid 1980s. The building, including the adjoining premises that was once Ayres bakery shop, survive today. All have since been renovated.

Guildford Indoor Market was a novel idea that enabled small retailers to set up shop in a town centre where rents and rates are known to be exceptionally high. The market was in premises formerly used by the Guildford and District Co-operative Society in Haydon Place.

There were shops selling clothing, records, jewellery, pet foods and even a barbers in the indoor market that lasted for several years. In 1989 the buildings in which it was held made way for new flats, offices and shop units.

The Woolworth store that was built on the site of the Lion Hotel in the High Street opened in 1957. It closed in 1984 when the site was redeveloped as the White Lion Walk shopping mall. In 1993 Woolworth returned to the town and took over the former Tesco store in Friary Street.

In November 1981 the town bridge was found to be dangerously corroded and had to be replaced. A temporary footbridge was put in its place while a new bridge, costing £250,000, was built to the form and width of the old one. These pictures show the new structure being lowered into place on a Sunday morning in 1985. Once completed, it was officially opened by the Mayor, Jack Patrick, and Surrey County Councillor Tom Waring.

The Co-op dairy in Woodbridge Road has now been replaced by a Currys and a PC World superstore. During the 1960s the Weyside Club had stood between the dairy and Eagle Caravans. It was an over 18s club with an emphasis on table tennis.

The Bridge Cafe and houses in Ladymead are boarded up awaiting their fate. They made way for the Ladymead Retail Park, that includes Sainsbury's Homebase, B&Q, and Burger King, among others.

Ladymead in 1986 looking east towards the Cornhill Insurance offices. How this scene has changed!

Bridge House seen from Farnham Road in October 1987 shortly before it was knocked down. Built in the early 1960s, it was initially used by the Post Office as its area telephone headquarters. A new Bridge House was built in its place and is currently home for the Government Office for the South East.

A view from the top of what is now the Wey House building beside the gyratory system in Park Street. This is the late 1980s and now more than a decade later there have been a number of changes. The Rodboro Buildings have been renovated, some of the shops seen here in Bridge Street have been converted into bars while the once well-known Guildford coach firm Blue Saloon, has disappeared.

All change at the railway station. This shows the demolition of the station buildings that had stood for about 100 years. The rubble in the foreground is all that remains of the original Bridge House. The new railway station has won a design award.

The 1960s building at the foot of Portsmouth Road, formerly home to the Central Electricity Generating Board, was pulled down in 2000. Previously the site had been occupied by Lascelles Tickner & Co's Castle Brewery and later Guildford Glass Works.

The gyratory system in the late 1980s as it dives under Friary Court. Today, Debenhams, on the far right, is undergoing some alterations, while the Sydenham Road multi-storey car park seen here (top left) is being replaced by a new one.

The Great Storm of Friday, October 16, 1987, lasted only three hours, but it changed the landscape in many parts of Southern England. Thousands of trees were uprooted and came crashing to the ground. If you were not woken by the growling hurricane-force wind, you certainly saw its effects the following morning. The 70ft Booker's Tower, on the side of The Mount near Guildown, could suddenly be seen from miles around.

Two noted trees at the Castle Cliffe Gardens fell victim to the Great Storm. The curator of Guildford Museum, Matthew Alexander, looks at the fallen Judas tree. It was planted at the turn of the 20th century by the owner of the Wey Navigations, William Stevens. The other tree that fell was a chestnut – the last of a row that gave their name to the house lived in by Lewis Carrol's sisters.

Many surrounding areas lost power as electric cables were brought down during the storm. Engineers were drafted in from all over the UK to repair the damage. Roads were blocked and it was several months before all the debris was cleared away. This view shows the Wood Bridge area of Woodbridge Road looking towards Ladymead.

# *Shalford*

Barges with collapsible masts on the Godalming Navigation at Stonebridge Wharf. Like the turnpiked roads, this waterway also lost out to the railways. However, in its heyday it transported all manner of goods ranging from building materials, flour, paper and chalk for liming, to gunpowder manufactured at Chilworth.

Shalford Mill on the River Tillingbourne in the 1870s with its mill pond, now long gone. The mill dates from the 18th century. It was last used as a working mill in 1914. In 1932 it was rescued by a band of preservationists known as Ferguson's Gang and converted into a house. It is now a National Trust property.

Charles Warn, his wife Isobella, and their children Rose, William and Herbert, lived in Shalford. He worked for an electrical generator firm but it was his son, William (right), who founded Warn's Garage which is still trading today. Herbert also worked at the garage.

William Warn started his motor-car and cycle repair business in the early part of the 20th century. His brother Herbert (centre) stands in front of the original Kings Road premises.

A wonderful composition of East Shalford Lane by the Albury photographer Percy Lloyd. The elderly gentleman appears to be warning the dog not to move while the picture is being taken. It was published as a postcard and dates from about 1905.

Shalford House was originally the residence of the Austen family but became an hotel with its own golf course from 1910 to 1938. During World War Two it was used as offices by Cornhill Insurance. It was pulled down in the 1970s to make way for the River Wey abstraction scheme. The site is presently occupied by Thames Water.

The enamel signs are advertising Lipton's tea and R. White's mineral waters but the little shop and post office along the Shalford Road would have stocked all manner of provisions.

Kings Road and the village pond in the early 1900s. Among the parade of shops was once a tearoom called Rolanders and on the far right can be seen the Surrey Trading Company which later became the Forest Stores.

*Right:* R. White's had enamel advertising signs on village and corner shops throughout the South East of England. Robert White started his mineral water business in Camberwell in 1845. By the time his sons had taken over at the end of the 19th century it had further factories and depots in Kingston, Croydon, Windsor and Stoke Road, Guildford.

Children stand on the common with Savill's Broadford Brewery and the Parrot Inn in the background. The brewery had been founded by Frederick Webb in the 1860s although brewing had been going on here for several years previously. In 1891 he sold it along with the Parrot Inn to Ebenezer Savill for £8,700. When Mr Savill died it was taken over by Cobham United Breweries. Brewing ceased in 1913 when it became a laundry. This burned down in 1923 and four years later the site was developed as the Vulcanised Fibre Works. During World War Two fuel tanks for Spitfire aeroplanes were made here. The factory closed in 1967 and a modern business park occupies much of the site today.

A picturesque view of Chantry Cottage, off Pilgrims Way, during a snowy Edwardian winter. It was formerly a keeper's cottage on Shalford's Austen Estate.

Savill & Co Ltd, one pint beer bottle, circa 1910.

# St Catherine's

For centuries there has been a crossing point of the River Wey at St Catherine's. Travellers on the primeval Terrace-way would arrive from the direction of the Hog's Back. During the 1930s drinks and snacks could be bought, including large arrow-root biscuits, from a hut beside the river. A ferry operated until 1963.

St Catherine's Lock surrounded by water meadows in Edwardian times. To the far left can be seen the semaphore signals on the railway line at the start of Peasmarsh Junction. The canal cuts an almost straight line through the water meadows while the river meanders off to the right. This area was once known as Three Oaks and was a popular place for swimmers.

Further upstream still, a cottage on the banks of the Godalming Navigation.

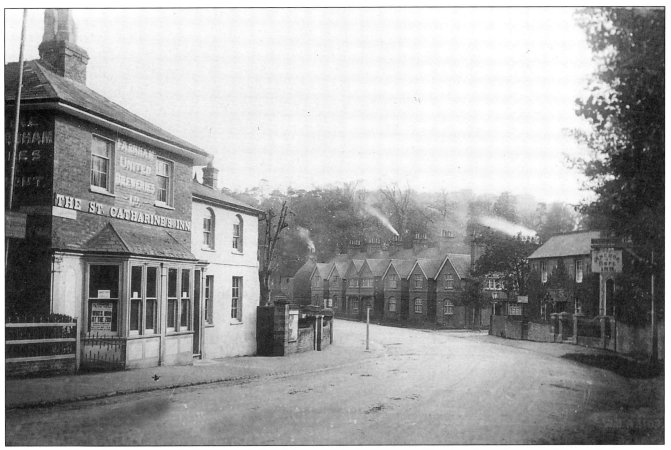

A picture of the public house on the Portsmouth Road that once had two names. The sign above the ground floor windows reads St Catharine's Inn (note the unique spelling) while on the opposite side of the road a hanging sign claims it as the Anchor and Hope. Seen here in the early 1900s, it sold ale brewed by Farnham United Breweries Ltd. However, by World War Two it had become a private residence.

The covered wagon is passing The Ship Inn, thought to have once been called The Red Lion. At the turn of the 20th century it was owned by Hodgsons' Kingston Brewery.

Not all Edwardian picture postcard views were photographs. There were many artist-drawn cards. This watercolour painting by Edwin Noble was published by A. C. Curtis, whose High Street shop sold all manner of items including toys and picture frames. Today his premises has become the borough's art gallery, Guildford House. The ruins of St Catherine's Chapel date from the 14th century.

During the early years of the 20th century Ferry Lane and the St Catherine's area was well photographed by postcard companies. This is a most delightful view of the picturesque row of cottages and its occupants.

# Merrow and Burpham

The forge at Merrow must have been something of a landmark building with its horseshoe-shaped doorway. It was demolished in 1955 and a petrol station built in its place.

The Horse and Groom public house has served ales under the name of the Running Horse and before that the Hare and Hounds. Although there is a date of 1615 on the front of the building, experts suggest that it was not built until 1650 and was originally a farm house. From 1864 until 1938 it was owned by the Reigate brewers Mellersh & Neale who used a picture of Reigate castle as their trade mark.

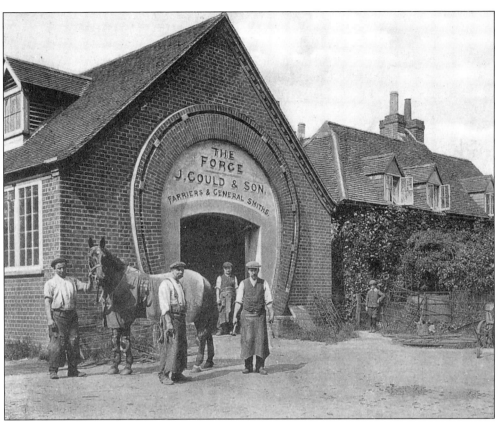

An almost deserted Epsom Road in Edwardian times. The second building from the left with the bay window was once a post office and general stores.

Most of the houses in Down Road were built in the 1880s. It was originally called New Down Road and about half-way up on the east side was a primary school for local children. This view dates from about 1910.

This late 1930s view of Epsom Road shows the Walnuts Cafe on the right. Other shops included Masseys the chemist, Kimber & Sons bakers, and Stoke Hill & Lee Farm Dairies. The bus shelter looks brand new!

Merrow Street, which now runs through Merrow Park estate, was once a country lane complete with its own 'village' pond. It is seen here a few years before World War Two.

Now tucked away off the main A25, this is Black Cottage which dates back to the 18th century.

Newlands Corner, with its spectacular views across the Weald to the South Downs, has been a popular rendezvous for locals and day trippers, even before motor-cars, as this 1900s view shows.

This small thatched hut was the Christy Kiosk at Newlands Corner. Besides serving teas, ices and mineral waters, picture postcards of the surrounding area could also be purchased. A customer appears to be looking at a selection of these in this 1920s view.

Once called Newlands Farm, the building was a restaurant when this photo was taken in the 1920s. It still stands today near the Manor Hotel.

The Kingpost swimming pool and restaurant at Burpham with an interesting line of cars seen top right. The complex opposite the Green Man public house began as the Astolat Garden Shop and then became the Kingpost Restaurant. The swimming pool venture did not take off and it closed at about the time of World War Two. Some of the buildings were then used as a church and other uses have included a drawing office, a caravan showroom and a car showroom.

Home Guardsmen of B Company 4th (Guildford) Battalion Surrey Home Guard, whose job it was to patrol the Merrow and Burpham area during World War Two. The Home Guard comprised of men who were either too old to be called up for the armed services or who worked in a reserved occupation. The Guildford Battalion's motto was adopted using the four Is – Invisibility, Inaudibility, Individuality and Initiative.

The Green Man at Burpham, with its Paddock Rooms, in 1984 shortly before it was turned into a Harvester restaurant. At this time the pub still had an outside ladies lavatory.

Following the Great Storm of October 1987 a crowd has gathered in Horseshoe lane, Merrow, as a tree is sawn up. With fallen timber everywhere it was soon realised that some of it could be very valuable. Surrey farmers were advised to pool their timber to get the best prices. 'Think before you saw logs', was one piece of advice. It was estimated that an oak tree could be worth £100.

# Worplesdon & Wood Street Village

A. M. Young and Co's Rickford Mill, pictured in about 1920. In the book *Old Surrey Water Mills*, published in 1951, the author, J. Hillier, wrote that in conversation with the miller there he found that he had a marked preference for cog wheels made of hornbeam. Those made of apple, oak, or anything else he denounced would all split: 'All of 'em, but not hornbeam'.

Cricket on the green at Worplesdon, but which green? This is in fact the area of land bordering the A322 and Gooserye Road at the bottom of Rickford Hill. The present sports ground and the Memorial Hall were established after World War One. This open space is now covered with trees.

Have they lost the ball? These look to be the same spectators seen in the previous picture. The view looks up Rickford Hill.

Both the Avenue, going off to the right, and the main road through Worplesdon look in fairly good condition in this view from about 1920. Were the piles of stones left by the road side used to fill in pot holes?

The public house at the top of Perry Hill started out in the 17th century as the White Lyon. In 1718 it became the New Inn. It is seen here in the early 1900s and was pulled down at the end of the 1930s. A new roadhouse-style pub was built in its place – presumably to attract the ever increasing motor trade. The pub became the White Lyon again in 1966.

Something seems to have caught the attention of the black dog sitting outside the New Inn. This view, to the cottages across the green, has hardly changed except that today there is a line of horse chestnut trees beside the road.

The origins of the Church of St Mary the Virgin go back to Norman times, although much 'vandalism' was done when a group of Victorians set about restoring the building in 1866. Many original features were lost including a Norman font which was replaced by one from Eton College.The rector from 1931-42, the Rev G. J. Chitty, learned of this loss and appealed for its return suggesting that local farmers may have unsuspectingly been using it as a drinking trough for their cattle. Unfortunately, the square black marble font was never returned.

See how narrow the road at Perry Hill once was as it passed the school. Note the tall hedges on either side.

Looking across the green at Pitch Place in about 1910. The white building at the end of the row is the Ship Inn. Guildford architects Lunn & Hodgson designed the present pub for the Friary Brewery. They also designed the Anchor and Horseshoes public house at Burpham.

An unrecognisable Pitch Place with H. Hooker's Stores, and on the far left the original Ship public house.

Pitch Place looking towards Stoughton. The post office (with enamel advertising signs on its wall) and the terrace cottages survive, but the buildings in the left foreground have been pulled down. The forecourt of a motor garage now occupies the site.

High summer and a view looking west along Frog Grove Lane in Wood Street Village. Between the two wars a ribbon of development took place through to Clasford Bridge.

Telegraph poles 'march' up the road to Oak Hill. This view dates from the 1930s when the houses, set back across the common, were new. The village school on the opposite side of the road had opened in 1878.

The Wood Street Church Mission Hall, made of timber and asbestos on brick foundations with a corrugated iron roof, was dedicated on June 20, 1925. Central heating was installed the following year. It was rededicated St Alban's Church in 1937 and replaced by today's church in 1967. The clock survived and today can be seen on the wall of the Guildford Horological Workshops in Worplesdon Road, Stoughton.

The Jolly Farmer Inn along Burdenshott Road was a Lascelles Tickner & Co public house and when this photograph was taken the licensee was a J. Burtenshaw. As the sign on the cart reads, he was also a coal merchant, with Worplesdon railway station given as his address.

# Stoughton

Shepherds Lane, long before houses were built on either side. On the right can be seen the Emmanuel Church vicarage which was completed in May 1908. At the end of the lane on the left can be seen one of the round houses and in the distance the roofs and chimneys of Stoughton Barracks. The large oak tree on the right survived until comparatively recently. Locally the lane has been called Vicarage Lane and Clark's Lane, after the farmer at Shepherd's Farm in the 1880s.

Emmanuel Church was consecrated on October 13, 1902, and replaced an iron church which stood on the opposite side of Worplesdon Road. Its first vicar was the Rev Henry John Burkitt who had been vicar-designate since 1892. He remained until September 1918. In 1990, under the present vicar – the Rev Canon John Salter – the church was enlarged due to an ever increasing congregation. Church building specialists Ogilvie & Gardner of Littlehampton, West Sussex, undertook the work. Finally, the church got a spire which had been part of the original design.

Looking up Worplesdon Road towards Emmanuel Church with Sparrow the butcher's shop on the right. Established in 1880, it had its own slaughter house – the entrance was through the wooden gates seen next to the flag pole. The Shepherds Hill council houses had not been built when this photo was taken, dating it to the years prior to World War One.

Sparrow the Butcher's delivery cart.

The line of houses and shops on the east side of Worplesdon Road were once known to locals as Stoughton High Street. The women and children look like they are dressed in their Sunday best, perhaps on their way to church. They are passing the barber's shop that was run by Frederick Reed.

The charabanc's canvas hood has been drawn up and it looks like the weather is going to be wet as this group of Stoughtonians prepare to depart on a day trip. E. W. Lyons who owned the shop on the corner of Baden Road sold all manner of items and also repaired bicycles and motor vehicles.

In the days before retail parks and superstores it would seem there was a shop on every street corner. This is Worplesdon Road in the early 1920s. Annie Gowing's grocers and confectionery shop had plenty of advertising signs to entice customers. It was also something of a meeting place with boys from the local football team retiring there after matches; no doubt to have a cup of tea and post-game chat.

Years after Gowing's shop had closed, the author retrieved two of the shop's enamel advertising signs seen here. One was found behind the gas cooker in the house next-door, the other had been dumped in the back alley.

Edwardian wedding: Dan and Rose Chesterman were married in 1906. The photograph was taken in the back yard of the off licence in Worplesdon Road, on the corner with Percy Road. It was run by the bride's mother, Mrs Crawt. Note the women's hats and that all the men have removed their own caps for the photograph. Cabbages have been planted out and bean poles are propped up against the fence. The building looks practically the same today.

The impressive keep and entrance to Stoughton Barracks, home to The Queen's Regiment, was built in 1876. The Queen's left the barracks in 1959 when it amalgamated with other units. The buildings were then used by the pay corps until 1983, becoming derelict until the 1990s when the site was redeveloped for homes by Countryside Residential plc. It is now called Cardwells Keep after Edward Cardwell, a War Secretary, who in the 1870s had chosen the site when the Army was reorganised on a county basis. The keep itself, the officers' mess and several other accommodation blocks were converted into homes with many new houses built around them.

The men's quarters were standard barrack blocks of the period – quite imposing and solid. The bricks had been made locally by W. Henley of Pitch Place. After their 1990s refurbishment, a two-bedroom second-floor apartment in the keep was offered for £91,950, while a three-bedroomed end of terrace property with garage in Queen Elizabeth Mews – formerly soldiers' accommodation like the buildings seen here – was on the market for £118,950.

Facing the parade ground was the barrack's hospital. It was pulled down to make way for the Cardwells Keep redevelopment.

The officers' mess has since been converted into homes and is now called King George's Lodge. The author, who went to Stoughton Infant and Junior Schools next door, remembers a door in the barrack's wall that could be used when a ball was kicked over it from the playground. In the early 1970s access to the barracks was unchallenged. The author remembers spending summer evenings playing with school friends some of whom were the children of servicemen. However, one evening a soldier told him in no uncertain terms to leave the premises immediately. The troubles were escalating in Northern Ireland and risks to security were feared. A strict guard was then put on the barrack's gates.

Stoughton post office was once located here in Barrack Road. Further along was a bakery and on the opposite side of the road the Soldiers' Welcome. This was a non-alcoholic alternative to the bar of the Royal Hotel. It was established courtesy of Julia Paynter, the wife of the Rev Francis Paynter, in 1904. It was open during the evenings between 6pm and 9.30pm and to the soldiers' wives on Friday afternoons. Renovation work on the house in recent years revealed the original hand-painted sign above the front door.

Looking like something out of a fairy story this was one of several roundhouses that once stood in the Stoughton area. Built as lodges for Stoughton Place Estate, this one was on the north side of Grange Road, beyond Grange Farm. A figure can just be seen standing in the shadows of the doorway.

Grange Farm, Stoughton, seen in the early 1900s. This is roughly where the entrance to Little Street, off Grange Road, is today. The barn still stands.

From 1924 the Butcher family owned Grange Farm, eventually selling it to the Burdens. Many will remember buying ice creams from the dairy which faced on to Grange Lane.

In 1890 the Methodist circuit of Guildford bought a plot of land on the corner of Grange Road and Stoughton Road and erected an iron-clad church room as a temporary place of worship. Within five years enough funds had been raised and the present church was opened. Little has changed in this view and even the blue enamel street sign for Grange Road is still in situ high up on the church wall.

Cyclists make their way up Manor Road from Woodbridge Hill in this Edwardian view. The parade of shops here included a dairy.

Manor Road, Stoughton, looking north. The villas on the west side of the road look the same today. In the early 1900s a tall hedge on the opposite side bordered Mosnor, later Manor Lodge – the home of the Rev Robert Ransom, curate of Stoke from 1885-90. This building and Ardmore House, also in Manor Road, had been demolished by the 1960s and flats built in their place.

Stoughton Brass and Reed Band pictured during Guildford's celebrations for the coronation of George V in 1911. The band took part in the official programme of events. A souvenir booklet lists the band playing a promenade concert from 11am to 12.15pm in the High Street at the junction of London and Merrow (Epsom) Roads and from 6pm to 7pm in North Street opposite the fire station. The conductor was Mr J. Hammond, Bandmaster. The programme included *The Lost Chord, Evening Bells, Under Sunny Skies,* and *Flying Fox* among a total of 11 tunes.

Completed in 1907, the Caxton Gardens Housing Scheme was built for employees of the Billings printing works in Walnut Tree Close.

Anyone for tennis? The residents of Caxton Gardens were certainly up for a game in years gone by. They were really rather competitive organising matches against other streets in the Woodbridge Hill area. It seems to be a glorious summer's day in this view which looks to date from the 1920s.

The Woodbridge Hill premises of The Guildford Stores in about 1920. The right-hand window is stocked with Christmas crackers. Note the signs for Birds Egg Custard, Cadbury's chocolate, Marmite and Bovril. For poorer people meat extracts such as Bovril were an important part of their diet. Bovril was first sold in Canada in 1874, and when its inventor, Jim Johnston, moved to London in 1886, it went on sale here.

Two early 20th century Bovril jars (centre) with rival brands Borthwick's and the Co-op Wholesale Society's Extract of Meat.

Woodbridge Hill in the 1920s with the London Stores (formerly the Guildford Stores) on the corner of Weston Road. This later became Pride's greengrocers. Other shops which once occupied this parade included Austin the butcher's; Hay the fishmonger and Battersby & Sons, ironmongers.

A steam train hurtling over the bridge at the foot of Woodbridge Hill has attracted some attention. The date is about 1920 and the white sign post is pointing in the direction of the isolation hospital located at the end of the road that ran past Dennis Bros motor works.

Nicknamed the Happy Family, the Yellow Bus Services ran from 1920 until 1958, linking the Stoughton, Rydes Hill and Bellfields areas with Guildford. It also operated to Camberley via Ash and Farnham via Puttenham. Seen in Barrack Road, this is the firm's 14-seater Chevrolet that it acquired from new in 1924.

The YBS staff in front of their vehicles at the Worplesdon Road garage during the 1930s. Back row from left: Arthur Mosdell, Cecil Davies, Tom Street, Harold Fletcher, Jim Wadsworth, Pat Russell, Fred Barnes. Front row: Percy Lawes, Ernie Glew, Arthur Bowden, Dick Seymour and Alf Whitfield.

Seen here in Worplesdon Road, a YBS vehicle decorated for the parade through the town on the occasion of Queen Elizabeth II's coronation in 1953. Much of the decorative work was made by local hairdresser George Yates of Maison George. The person sitting in the chariot on top of the bus is Ann Tizard (née Leonard).

The YBS had been founded by a Frank Hutchins. He was partnered by Sydney Hayter who later ran the business until he died in 1951. After his death his widow allowed the firm's stalwart employee Ernie Glew to carry on as manager. Although the little yellow buses with their friendly crews were not seen after June 15, 1958 – when it had been taken over by the Aldershot & District Traction Co – the YBS service station continued for many years. It is seen here on the corner of Worplesdon Road with New Cross Road in the 1960s.

Guildford was one of the first towns to provide nursery schools in prefabricated buildings. By 1942 it had five centres — Stoughton, Westborough, Rectory Place, St Nicolas Hall and Merrow. They catered for 180 children with another 100 on the waiting list. The picture shows meal time at Stoughton Nursery Centre, Northmead.

Although the exact location is unknown this is a group of people from the Stoughton area on an excursion – probably to the Sussex coast, standing by one of the yellow buses in the early 1950s.

# Stoke

The original version of this photograph is labelled Stoke Malthouse. These buildings stood on the site of the present Rowbarge public house at Riverside, on the edge of today's Bellfields Estate. The roof on the far right is almost certainly the miller's house at Stoke Mill. The picture dates from the 1870s by which time the malthouse had been divided into tenements.

Woking Road in the early 1900s with the Bell public house which dates back to the middle of the 19th century. On the right is Stoke Mission Church, now used as commercial premises.

Stoke Lock on the Wey Navigations was at one time an isolated place which was just as well as during the late Victorian and Edwardian period Guildford's rubbish was tipped beside the riverbank a few hundred yards from here. The refuse came by barge from the council's Bedford Road depot.

Stoke Mills pictured shortly after the current Stoke Bridges were constructed in 1926. There have been mills at Stoke since the time of the Domesday Book. The single-storey building was built as a paper mill in 1863 while the four-storey mill dates from 1879. Owned for many years by the Bowyer family, the last corn was milled in 1957. Grant & West then took over the building as a paint and chemicals factory/warehouse. In 1989 it was fully restored as office accommodation and became the headquarters of the *Surrey Advertiser* in 1999. The newspaper group's titles are printed outside the county in Reading.

The two single-storey buildings here were lodge cottages at the Woking Road entrance to the Stoke Hill House and estate which was owned by the Paynter family. In 1944 the 184-acre estate was bought by Guildford Borough Council for £42,000. Bellfields Estate was built here and was one of the first of its kind in the UK to have open-plan frontage to the homes.

A rare photograph of Stoke Hill House. There were plans to turn it into a community centre but they came to nothing and so it was pulled down in the 1950s.

The tower of St John the Evangelist Church at Stoke seen from the graveyard on the opposite side of Stoke Road at about the turn of the 20th century. Within a few years of this photo being taken the diamond-shaped clock face had been replaced by a round-faced design.

The old Stoke Rectory pictured in the 1920s when it was in use as a guest house. Dating from about 1800 it was originally known as The Parsonage. With the rector of Stoke, the Rev Francis Paynter, living at Stoke Hill House, the rectory became home to a number of curates during the second half of the 19th century. It stood opposite the fire station.

It really could be anywhere but this is in fact the tree-lined Woodbridge Avenue, now the Ladymead end of Woodbridge Road.

Not even The Guildford Society's vigorous protests could save Stoke Park House from demolition in 1977. Internally, it was in a fair condition having been used as a school until World War Two. It then became part of Guildford Technical College. This view would appear to date from the 1900s.

The main staircase inside Stoke Park House in about 1920 when it was in use as a school.

The lodge to Stoke Park House still stands today but the entrance to the park and lido has been relocated further along Stoke Road.

In 1881 Stoke Model Farm was created off Nightingale Road, previously New Road, by the then owner of Stoke Park House James Smith Budgett. He was the head of a sugar brokers in London and was on the board of management of the Royal Surrey County Hospital. These buildings have changed little and the stable blocks have for many years been used as sports changing rooms.

'Isn't this a pretty spot? We took the little boy next door here on Monday to sail his yacht,' begins the message on the back of this 1930s picture postcard. The yachting pool is still a popular area of Stoke Park although today it is easy to overlook the original Japanese style of the gardens, which was much more evident when they were created.

Several generations of Guildfordians have enjoyed a day out at the Lido. It was built in 1933 and although under threat of closure in recent years, its annual opening is looked forward to by many, along with the hopes of a long hot summer.

# Bibliography

*A Brush with Steam – David Shepherd's Railway Story*, David Shepherd. (David & Charles, Newton Abbot, 1990).

*Antiquities of Surrey,* Surrey County Council. (SCC, Kingston upon Thames, 1965).

*Bellfields Remembered – An Oral History*, Bellfields Oral History Group. (Parchment Oxford Ltd. Oxford, 1999).

*Branch Lines to Horsham*, V. Mitchell, K. Smith. (Middleton Press, Midhurst, 1984).

*Burpham, Norman Manor to Suburban Village*, Roger Marjoribanks. (Roger Marjoribanks, 1997).

*Cardwells Keep,* housing development brochure. (Countryside Residential plc).

*Cycle Speedway in South West Surrey*, R. Richardson. (self published booklet, Dorking, Surrey).

*Discovering Picture Postcards,* C. W. Hill. (Shire Publications, 1970).

*General &Business Guide to Guildford,* (Walser & Grist, London and Hove, 1892).

*Guildford A Biography*, E. R. Chamberlin. (Macmillan & Co. Ltd. London, 1970).

*Guildford A Pictorial History,* Shirley Corke. (Phillimore & Co. Ltd, 1990).

*Guildford A Short History,* Matthew Alexander. (Ammonite Books, Godalming, 1992).

*Guildford A Photographic Record,* John Janaway. (Ammonite Books, Godalming, 1990).

*Guildford As It Was,* Matthew Alexander. (Hendon Publishing, Lancashire, 1978).

*Guildford Cathedral*, Pitkin Pride of Britain Books and Colour Souvenirs. (Pitkin Pictorials Ltd. London, 1980).

*Guildford High School. The First Hundred Years 1888-1988*, (Guildford High School, 1988).

*Guildford The War Years – 1939-45*, G. Collyer, D. Rose. (The Breedon Books Publishing Company, Derby, 1999).

*Guildford Town Under Siege,* Russell Chamberlin. (The Guildford Society, 1987).

*Happy Family – The Story of the Yellow Bus Services Stoughton*, N. Hamshere, J. Sutton. (1978).

*Images of Guildford*, G. Collyer, D. Rose. (The Breedon Books Publishing Company, Derby, 1998).

*Kelly's Directory of Guildford, Godalming and Neighbourhood.* (Kelly's Directories Ltd. London, various years).

*Looking Back...,* Co-op Membership & Education Department. (Pinpoint, London, 1992).

*Merrow the Village and the Downs,* Louise Lewis. (Louise Lewis, 1998).

*Newlands Corner and its Environs,* Derek Nightingale. (Derek Nightingale, 1994).

*Official Programme of Guildford's Celebration of the Coronation of King George V June 22nd 1911*, (Borough of Guildford).

*Old Surrey Water Mills,* J. Hillier. (Sheffington & Son Ltd, London, 1951).

*Reading to Guildford*, V. Mitchell, K. Smith. (Middleton Press, Midhurst, 1988).

*Safeguard of Guildford 1924-1984 Diamond Jubilee A Pictorial Review,* J. Sutton, N. Hamshere. (1984)

*Shalford, Portrait of a Surrey Parish,* (Shalford Parish Council,1995).

*Stoke Next Guildford, A Short History*, Lyn Clarke. (Phillimore & Co Ltd, Chichester, 1999).

*Stoughton, Guildford People and Places,* Anne Sankey. (Commercial Press, Guildford).

*The Art of the Label,* Robert Opie. (Simon & Schuster, London, 1990).

*The Best of British Buses No. 4. 75 Years of Aldershot & District*, Alan Townsin. (The Transport Publishing Company, Glossop, Derbyshire, 1981).

*The Breweries and Public Houses of Guildford*, M. Sturley. (Charles W. Traylen, Guildford, 1990).

*The Breweries and Public Houses of Guildford Part Two*, M. Sturley. (M. Sturley, Guildford, 1995).

*The Guild Hall of Guildford and its Treasures,* Dr G. C. Williamson. (1928).

*The Guildford Guy Riots,* Gavin Morgan. (Northside Books, London, 1992).

*The Story of Onslow Village*, Helen Chapman Davies. (Helen Chapman Davies, 1999).

*The Story of Stoughton.* (The Church Publishers, Ramsgate, 1962).

*The Story of Stoughton – by Pen and Camera,* Rev Henry J. Burkitt. (Biddle & Shippam, Guildford, 1910).

*The Surrey Weather Book*, Mark Davison, Ian Currie. (Frosted Earth, 1990).

*Woking to Portsmouth,* V. Mitchell, K. Smith. (Middleton Press, Midhurst, 1996).

*Wood Street, The Growth of a Village,* Wood Street Village History Society. (Wood Street Village History Society, 1988).

*Worplesdon Old and New,* Joan Dingle in collaboration with Joan Tovey.